A Woman God Can Use

Pam Farrel

D1166059

HARVEST HOUSE PUBLISHERS
Eugene, Oregon 97402

Unless otherwise indicated, all Scripture quotations are taken from the Holy Bible, New International Version®. Copyright © 1973, 1978, 1984 by the International Bible Society. Used by permission of Zondervan Publishing House. The "NIV" and "New International Version" trademarks are registered in the United States Patent and Trademark Office by International Bible Society.

Verses marked NKJV are taken from the New King James Version, Copyright © 1979, 1980, 1982 by Thomas Nelson, Inc., Publishers. Used by permission.

Verses marked NASB are taken from the New American Standard Bible, © 1960, 1962, 1963, 1968, 1971, 1972, 1973, 1975, 1977, 1995 by The Lockman Foundation. Used by permission.

Verses marked NCV are taken from the *International Children's Bible, New Century Version,* Copyright © 1986, 1988 by Word Publishing, Dallas, Texas 75039. Used by permission.

Verses marked THE MESSAGE are taken from *The Message.* Copyright © 1993, 1994, 1995, 1996. Used by permission of NavPress Publishing Group.

Cover by Terry Dugan Design, Minneapolis, Minnesota

To contact Pam Farrel, write:
629 S. Rancho Santa Fe #306
San Marcos, CA 92069
(760) 727-9122

A WOMAN GOD CAN USE

Copyright © 1999 by Pam Farrel
Published by Harvest House Publishers
Eugene, Oregon 97402

Library of Congress Cataloging-in-Publication Data
  Farrel, Pam, 1959–
      A woman God can use / Pam Farrel.
   Includes bibliographical references.
   ISBN 0-7369-0071-3
   1. Christian women—Religious life.   2. Success—Religious aspects—Christianity.   I. Title.
BV4527.F48   1999
248.8'43—dc21   99-21975
                                                                                                              CIP

All rights reserved. No portion of this book may be reproduced in any form without the written permission of the Publisher.

Printed in the United States of America

00 01 02 03 / BP / 10 9 8 7 6 5 4 3 2

Contents

To all the women God has brought across my path,
My place in His plan is fulfilling
Because you are tools in God's hands
Helping to form me.

To the leaders I work shoulder to shoulder with,
Your love and encouragement
Keep me refreshed
As I serve in His place for me.

To Jim and Sally Conway,
Your wisdom has kept me usable
And your love has kept me secure
In His place rather than my own.

To my husband Bill,
Your time, talent and tenacious love
Have been used by God to carry me
To a place of confidence in His plan.

To my children,
May you find your place
In God's plan
Because you have helped me
Discover mine.

1

Finding Your Place in His Plan

How am I supposed to know what's important?

It was a simple gathering of friends. All of us were standing in the kitchen and chatting, as women often do at a party. Our conversation had drifted to the subject of vital areas of need in women's lives. Just then, a friend, a successful businesswoman, grabbed my hand and with intensity said, "Pam, I know a book you should write. Women need a book that shows us how to be successful without being so hard on ourselves! I have a friend who listens to all those self-help tapes—you know the ones that say: 'You are the master of your own destiny. You can achieve anything. You are all powerful. You…you…you.' The focus is all wrong! She's been feeding herself for months on this junk, as though she is the god of her own universe or something. She thought it would help boost her self-esteem and empower her, but just the opposite has happened. She just keeps hearing how she can make all her own successes, and when she doesn't have the results the tapes promise she feels as though she is more of a failure than ever before. I think she's going to end up in a padded cell. She's driving herself to the edge of a nervous breakdown!"

That's where we live. There is a wave of women's empowerment material cresting, but most of it neither empowers nor frees us. Instead, we are burdened with the unrealistic expectation that we are supposed to ride every wave.

As I have traveled the past few years while speaking on women's issues I have come to some startling conclusions. The first I knew years ago: Women can do some incredible things with a little equipping, encouragement and inspiration. But I was surprised by the next conclusion. I speak to some of the most together, tenderhearted, loving, motivated women in the world. These women are responsible and hard working. Some are wonderful mothers, others are wonderful businesswomen or ministry-minded leaders, and they are all great friends and assets to their communities, yet they feel fragmented, unsure and discouraged. I think many of us can relate to them.

Many of us today also struggle with feeling as if we are one big disappointment to everyone. For the most part, we are exhausted as we frantically try to please everyone in our world: our husbands, our children, our parents, our bosses, our clients, our friends and our co-workers at work and in volunteer work—all while we're trying to please God. Sometimes we might even be trying to please ourselves, but we are usually very low on the list of priorities. I asked women in a survey who they feel they disappoint most often, and the choices included parents, husbands, children, friends, co-workers, bosses, volunteer or church leaders, themselves, and God. The overwhelming majority marked that they thought they disappointed God most often. That answer ran three to one to the second place answer. How can this be? If God created us, if God desires a friendship with us, if He really is all-sufficient and self-existent in and of Himself, then can it really be so easy to disappoint Him? Or could it be that we have a warped view of what He really expects from our lives, our relationships and us? Do you want to be a woman God can use, but you don't want to feel used up in the process?

The average woman today feels like her life is like a giant jigsaw puzzle. There are lots of important pieces—she is even convinced that there is a beautiful picture—but she's looking for the puzzle box lid because she's not sure where to start or what she's really aiming at.

The scary thing is that our lives are jam-packed with activity as we frantically try to balance all of life's demands. We are trying to please those around us, but most of the time we feel like we are always letting someone down. Are you one of these women? Do you feel like someone is disappointed in you even as you read the words on this page? Do you wonder if God is pleased with your life?

Mirror, Mirror

In the fairy tale *Snow White*, the queen kept checking in with a mirror to determine her standing in the community. *Mirror, Mirror on the wall, who's the fairest of them all?* When I was a little girl, I always despised the queen. She was dark, foreboding and selfish. But now I think that's what happens to women who look to a false standard to check on their significance. Every woman is looking in a mirror. The question is, what mirror are we using?

We might not stand in front of the mirror in our bathroom, asking "Mirror, Mirror…" but we do look around and compare ourselves to others: to women in books, magazines, movies or TV; to friends who are more talented in areas where we feel insecure; to mentors and public leaders to whom we ascribe the attributes of "the perfect Christian woman." Sometimes we even compare ourselves to us, 10 years ago, 20 years ago or more. Could it be that we need a new mirror?

I needed a new mirror because my expectations, others' expectations of me and God's expectations seemed to be all jumbled up together. I couldn't tell when realistic expectations stopped and unrealistic expectations started. My mirror was so warped that when I sat down to think and plan, my list grew; when others talked with me, my list grew; and even when I read the Bible it felt like God was making my To Do list longer and longer. Because my perspective was so distorted, I thought God's expectations of me were impossible to fulfill. I found myself consistently angry with God, even though I knew He loved me.

One of the most freeing experiences in my life was a set of quiet times I had many years ago. I tried to look God face to face and let Him be my mirror as I read passages where God describes people. I looked up all the times in the Bible where God says, "You are…" There are hundreds of passages that proclaim who He says we are. Then I made a list of the ones that seemed to be direct revelations of what He expects of us. The results gave me a new lease on life! A close friend even said to me, "Pam, what's different about you? You seem happier, less stressed…it's almost as though you aren't as frantic as usual. I don't know, but it seemed that you were trying so hard to make everyone happy all the time. Don't get me wrong. Everyone around you is still doing well and feeling great about you—no, maybe we're all feeling better too. It's like whatever God has done in your life has made you freer and that's allowed us to be freer too."

I thought that observation was pretty amazing because she hadn't known what I'd been studying in my quiet times that year. She wasn't saying I had been legalistic, judgmental or harsh before, because those characteristics have never been ones I thought were productive. What she was saying is that I discovered a gracious calling and it had impacted her life too. That is my hope for you. I hope you gain a wonderful fresh view of yourself as you look at His view of you. I truly believe women are more successful in life if they have an accurate view of God and a clear reflection of how God sees them.

The by-product from this vital connection with God is that we then can truly find, focus in on and fulfill His significant calling on our lives because we will know what truly is significant to Him. We will be women God can use because our lives will be usable.

Can We Really Have It All?

Sometimes we are our own worst enemy. Our expectations regarding ourselves can easily fall to one extreme or another. While some women are on welfare, on drugs, sleeping with men who aren't any good for them, ignoring their children and really aren't caring what anyone expects from them, most women fall in the other extreme—they care too much. Patsy Clairmont, author and Women of Faith conference speaker, says, "We wouldn't care so much what people thought of us if we realized how little they do!"[1] This concern over how other people view us feeds into the fact that we are our own harshest critics. I asked women to tell me their description of a woman who "has it all!" These are my favorites because they made me smile:

She is never running late or misplacing anything. Well, I can never be a woman who has it all then because there are days I hunt for car keys, lost cleats, the pancake spatula and sometimes my kids or husband!

She's unwrinkled. This one knocks all of us over 40 right out of the running.

Perfect figure. Okay, this one's tough because it keeps changing! Marilyn Monroe wore a size 16 and I think the super models today shop in the toddler section. Plus, isn't beauty supposed to be in the eye of the beholder? Maybe that's it—everyone needs to get special 3-D glasses and maybe then I'd have that elusive "perfect figure"!

Talented, gorgeous, wealthy, easy life, no job, mother of three well-adjusted kids. This one is a classic example of what we do to ourselves all the time—contradict our values. If I was talented and gorgeous with an easy life of wealth and I didn't work for the money, would I really have three *well-adjusted* kids? (And why three kids?) And if I were so wonderfully talented, wouldn't I want to use it in some way? Would I be well-adjusted if I had "an easy life"? I have experienced just the opposite. Those women who have gone through some hardship and come out on the other side are some of the easiest women to be around because they are low-maintenance women. Their expectations are grounded in the real world.

She's on top of the world. Everything always goes in her favor. Never fails. Never? Some of the women I have met, interviewed, or read about in history have had lives filled with failures and setbacks. Often those very failures became part of the fiber that formed them into a woman God could use in a significant way. Helen Keller was left a blind deaf-mute by a childhood illness. She definitely didn't have it all—she had almost nothing—yet she became one of the most famous women of this century because she overcame what seemed to be insurmountable obstacles. She gives a glimpse into her success, "When one door of happiness closes, another opens: but often we look so long at the closed door that we do not see the one which has been opened for us." In my own life, I have found that when I hit obstacles, failures and roadblocks, it is then that I am in the classroom of heaven and I learn more about who God is and who He says I am.

Someone who has a maid that someone else *pays for!* (This is my all-time favorite description of a woman who has it all and I think I hear a hearty *Amen!* rising from women across the world on that one!)

This one was followed closely with: *A woman who has plenty of babysitters.* But the one who sums up "the woman who has it all" wrote, *June Cleaver! You know the rest!* Oh yes, the June Cleaver-Clair Huxtible-Carol Brady-Martha Stewart syndrome. Every generation of TV watchers has their icons. The problem is some of the people we put on a pedestal are not even real women, and we really want to keep up there the ones who are. The real women, like Martha, Oprah and Kathy Lee, only give us a glimpse of their everyday lives. We don't walk in their shoes, so we don't really know all the choices, regrets and feelings they might be experiencing. Oprah Winfrey, who tops the American talk show circuit and sits at the helm of a $415 million dollar empire, said, "People think because you're on TV you have the world by a string. But I have struggled with my own self-value for many many years."[2] Often times, we simply glamorize these women and that makes the bar even higher that we must hurdle ourselves over.

The "Martha Stewart" Syndrome

Because we all have friends in our lives who seem to have a knack for creating a wonderful atmosphere around them, we somehow think that we must also have that same ability or we've failed. A friend with two small toddlers at home recently emailed me this letter to help us both "lighten up" a bit on our own expectations.

A Letter From Martha Stewart!
Monday, 9:00 A.M.

Hi Sandy,

This perfectly delightful note is being sent on paper I made myself to tell you what I have been up to. Since it snowed last night, I got up early and made a sled with old barn wood and a glue gun. I hand-painted it in gold leaf, got out my loom and made a blanket in peaches and mauves. Then to make the sled complete, I made a white horse to pull it from some DNA that I just had sitting around my craft room. By then, it was time to start making the place mats and napkins for my 20 breakfast guests. I'm serving the old standard Stewart twelve-course breakfast, but I'll let you in on a little secret: I didn't have time to make the table and chairs this morning, I used the ones I had on hand. Before I moved the table into the dining room, I decided to add just a touch of the holidays. So I repainted the room in pinks and stenciled gold stars on the ceiling.

Then, while the homemade bread was rising, I took antique candle molds and made the dishes (exactly the same shade of pink) to use for breakfast. These were made from Hungarian clay, which you can get in almost any Hungarian craft store. Well, I must run. I need to finish the buttonholes on the dress I'm wearing for the breakfast. I'll get out the sled and drive this note to the post office as soon as the glue dries on the envelope I'll be making. Hope my breakfast guests don't stay too long—I have 40,000 cranberries to string with bay leaves before my speaking engagement at noon. It's a good thing.

Love, Martha

PS. When I made the ribbon for this typewriter I used $\frac{1}{8}$ inch gauze. I soaked it in a mixture of white grapes and blackberries which I grew, picked and crushed last week just for fun!

I don't know who wrote this original caricature of Martha, but the author did understand the "Martha Stewart" syndrome of high expectations we have on ourselves. And in all fairness to the real Martha Stewart, she has done a wonderful job of releasing women to be creative and she's helped equip them with some very practical advice along the way. That is why she has been such a success.

The bigger question is: Why do we, as women, feel bad about ourselves when we see a woman using her God-given gifts and talents well? Why do we feel that if we are not doing the same thing in the same way that we must be a failure?

What Do We Think Is Significant?

I surveyed hundreds of women in several states and asked them to respond to some questions. One of the questions was: What is your definition of significance? Over half of those responding included in their definition the words: making a difference, impacting others or enacting some kind of a change. Half of the women also included that if something is significant it benefits others. About one in six also said that something significant was important or outstanding. About ten percent tagged on that if it were truly significant it had to have lasting/eternal value or it had to somehow please God. The words positive, special and meaningful were also commonly used in the definitions. About one-quarter of the respondents created a meaning that was more concrete to them. Below are a few of their definitions. Which do you connect with?

Enough and accomplishment

Adequate

Above average

Very unusual

When you feel good about yourself

Major, a really big deal

Being different

Having a purpose

100 percent

Significance is relational. The relationships that I have been able to invest in and make a mark on are what are really important. Of course, the most important relationship is my relationship with God.

Passionate to you

Superior

Exceptional, beyond ordinary

When I have finished something I worked very hard doing (giving birth was significant!)

An event worth retelling

Uplifting

Valuable or makes someone else feel valued

Something others honor

Has a large impact on many

A wow!

One respondent really took this a step further:

Significance is an influence or a life-changing experience like:

   Comfort when comfort is needed

   Support when support is needed

   Encouragement when encouragement is needed

Laughter when laughter is needed

Tears when tears are needed

To be there when needed

This poem is beautifully written and is a wonderful sentiment, as are most of the definitions I received. Some of you read the definitions above and knew instinctively how to apply them to life. Many of you, however, may have found the definitions intangible. For example, how would a woman *know* when and what was *needed*? I find that this is one of the most confusing issues in a woman's life. There are so many needs—how can one person fill them? What is average, let alone above average or superior? What exactly constitutes a wow! (Sometimes this is easier, because people will actually say the word *"Wow!"* when they hear of something amazing, special or meaningful.)

I especially liked these two:

I think everything I do as long as I let God lead me is significant.

Significance must be defined by who we are and not what we do. (And to that I say ditto! The premise of this book is to help us see ourselves as God does.)

The problem of seeing ourselves as the sum of our works, however, is epidemic. John Robinson and Geoffrey Godbey, authors of *A Time for Life*, note that "Many Americans have become virtual walking résumés, defining themselves only by what they do."[3] We are more than the sum total of our dossier. Os Guinness calls us all to replace: "You are what you do" with "Do what you are."[4] The goal of this book is to help you discover who and what you are, then make decisions based on that calling. This approach leads to wiser choices and a life where we sense God's pleasure—and that is significant.

Are you sensing why our heads are swimming? Why our Day-timers are jammed with To Do lists, why we might be feeling like we are very busy, yet wondering if we are accomplishing anything of value? Significance seems so subjective. What may seem significant to one may seem insignificant to another.

When I was a competitive gymnast and diver, I was judged by a panel of judges and then given a score. It was common for the same dive, the same vault or the same routine to receive a variety of scores. Each judge was receiving the same information, but a large or small mistake was subject to his/her view, his/her liking, his/her priorities. Significance is like that. So often we feel that our lives are being judged by a panel—husband, friends, leaders, church members, co-workers, bosses, children—and each of these people look at us from their own point of view. They are all subjective, so each gives us a different score.

The many voices judging our lives can feel like a distraction that is keeping us from asking the bigger question that might free us to truly sense the significant in life. The problem is, when you listen to too many voices, significance starts to become elusive, because then you don't know whom to please. God's view of you is concrete. Genuine significance is rooted and grounded in Him.

A significant woman bases her identity on who God says she is and she is committed to do nothing more and nothing less than what her identity demands. In other words, as I line up my thoughts to God's thoughts about me, I will become a woman God can use. When I see myself through God's eyes, I realize my value. I am nothing more than a woman saved by His grace, but I am nothing less than a new creation.

When I see myself through God's eyes, I realize God's plan for me is only found in obedience. I am nothing more than a servant and am nothing less than ambassador. I'm not the master, so I don't make up the rules. There is one God, and it's not me! All that God requires from a servant is obedience—there is nothing more

I can add. Being an ambassador opens up opportunities. The more God can trust me, the more He will entrust to me. So anything less than obedience means I risk missing out on precious pieces of His plan for me.

When I see myself through God's eyes, I realize my calling and that God has a unique place for me. If I am driven to do more than my calling, then I'm not being the me God designed. If in fear I do less than my calling, I miss out on the adventure of being me. Nothing more and nothing less will gain God's applause for me.

As I nurture the connection to God, I gain the desire, ability and motivation to obey. Out of obedience I will sense and experience a life of significance. When I agree with God's view of me, I gain the ability to grasp which opportunities are significant from heaven's vantage point. I see which relational connections are significant from God's box seat on high and even what daily, seemingly insignificant actions and decisions might have significant impact from an eternal perspective. As I see myself from God's point of view, the pieces fall together easier because God holds the box top to the puzzle. God sees the completed picture of me and my life. My relationship with God is the key that unlocks the puzzle's solution. Now, let's sort out the pieces—and find the framework for your life.

❀ ❀ ❀

Putting the Pieces Together

How would you describe a woman "who has it all"? How is the description different from your life right now?

You Are...

Sometimes we forget to look at ourselves through God's eyes. Place this list somewhere you can see it often. You are ...

The salt of the earth	
The light of the world	Matthew 5:13-14
More valuable than birds	Luke 12:24
In Me and I in you	John 14:20, 17:21
Already clean	John 15:3
The branches	John 15:5
My friends	John 15:14
Heirs of the prophets and of the covenant	Acts 3:25
Servants of the Most High	Acts 16:17
Called	Romans 1:6-7
Weak in your natural selves	Romans 6:19
Still worldly	1 Corinthians 3:2-4
God's fellow workers, God's field, and God's building	1 Corinthians 3:9
God's temple	1 Corinthians 3:16-17
Strong, Honored	1 Corinthians 4:10
A temple of the Holy Spirit	1 Corinthians 6:19
Standing firm	1 Corinthians 10:12-13
Part of the body of Christ	1 Corinthians 12:27
A letter from Christ	2 Corinthians 3:1-3
Christ's ambassador	2 Corinthians 5:20
Sons of God	Galatians 3:26
Abraham's seed	Galatians 3:28-29
Sons, an heir	Galatians 4:6-10
Children of the promise	Galatians 4:27-28
Fellow citizens and members of God's household	Ephesians 2:19
Children of the light	Ephesians 5:8
Standing firm	1 Thessalonians 3:8
Sons of the light and sons of the day	1 Thessalonians 5:4-5
Slow to learn	Hebrews 5:11
Mist	James 4:14
Living stones	1 Peter 2:5
A chosen people, a royal priesthood, and a holy nation	1 Peter 2:9-10
Daughters of Sarah	1 Peter 3:6

All the Wrong Places

Is one plan better than another?

Television talk-show host Chris Chubbuck wrote her own death script and carried it out by putting a gun to her head and pulling the trigger as viewers watched. The 29-year-old anchorwoman died in a hospital 14 hours later in Sarasota, Florida.

Her handwritten, blood-spattered script read, "Today Chris Chubbuck shot herself during a live broadcast." The story she had scrawled in longhand was found on the desk where she sat Monday and calmly announced to viewers what she said was a television first:

> In keeping with Channel 40's policy of bringing you the latest in blood and guts and in living color you are going to see another first—attempted suicide.

Then she reached into a shopping bag behind her desk, pulled out a .38 caliber revolver, fired a single shot and slumped forward.

Following the incident, the Sarasota sheriff's office and station WXLT were swamped with calls from viewers who could not believe the shooting had been real. It was real. A real woman, who seemed to be on top of the world, felt like she wasn't. Women everywhere on a daily basis make similar life-altering, self-destructive choices because the pieces of their lives seem to be falling apart. Maybe you have never put a gun to your head, but have you shortchanged yourself because you were afraid, unsure and insecure? Have you ever told yourself that happily-ever-afters are for other women, not you? Have you accepted the status quo rather than reaching up? Have you thought your dreams would come true if you were only smarter, taller, thinner or richer?

How Discontentment Began

That's how all this discontentment started. One woman knowing the plan, didn't believe it was the real key to happiness. One woman listened to some lies and believed them to be truth. One woman rejected God's view of significance and embraced a false promise. It sounded good, but it was bad—real bad. That woman was Eve.

One day after Eve had walked with God and enjoyed the perfect garden He had created for her and Adam, she stopped by to chat with a crafty serpent. He must have been charming, intriguing and engaging. He said to Eve, "Did God really say, 'You must not eat from any tree in the garden'?" Strike one.

Then Eve repeated the instructions she knew so well, "I am not to eat the fruit of this tree or I will die." So the serpent pulled out his most convincing lie: "You will not surely die," the serpent said to the woman. "For God knows that when you eat of it your eyes will be opened, and you will be like God, knowing good and evil." Strike two.

Then Eve acted on the wrong information. She knew it was the opposite of what God said. She was fully aware of her choice but unaware of its consequences. "When the woman saw that the fruit of the tree was good for food and pleasing to the eye, and also desirable for gaining wisdom, she took some and ate it. She also gave some to her husband, who was with her, and he ate it." Strike three—we're out!

The reality of it all hit. "Then the eyes of both of them were opened, and they realized they were naked; so they sewed fig leaves together and made coverings for themselves. Then the man and his wife heard the sound of the Lord God as he was walking in the garden in the cool of the day, and they hid from the Lord God among the trees of the garden.

"But the Lord God called to the man, 'Where are you?' and later God said to Eve, 'What is this you have done?'

"The woman said, 'The serpent deceived me, and I ate.'" And the consequences of her embrace of false significance have laid the foundation for all of us to be prone to the same deceptions.

God laid out the ramifications of her decision: "I will greatly increase your pains in childbearing; with pain you will give birth to children. Your desire will be for your husband, and he will rule over you." Only two sentences but they changed her life—and ours too. Just think about the "pain in childbirth" section. A woman begins her menstrual period in her mid teens. About once a month there are cramps and PMS with its symptoms of irritability, bloating, tension and anxiety. As we age, these symptoms often will worsen. We may get headaches, backaches and some-times even flu-like symptoms.

Then we have the joy (and discomfort) of housing another human being in pregnancy. After birth, our hormones can rage, baby blues can set in and weeks of melancholy and discontent-ment can overshadow the joy. Then menopause arrives and we wonder if we are losing our mind! We feel unplugged, unmoti-vated, unsure. Thanks a bunch Eve!

We are all prone to watching out for our own interests—and that's what got Eve into all this trouble in the first place. First John 2:15-16 lays out three similar ways we fall for false significance:

"Do not love the world or anything in the world. If anyone loves the world, the love of the Father is not in him. For every-thing in the world—(1) the cravings of sinful man, the (2) lust of his eyes and (3) the boasting of what he has and does—comes not from the Father but from the world." Our flesh wants to be fulfilled, then our eyes want what we see, then we want some-thing to brag about. Eve fell for the same three things. *It Feels So Good:* Her flesh wanted the fruit. *It Looks So Good:* Her eyes saw the new plan Satan laid out—and she wanted it. *It Sounds So Good:* Then she fell for the big one, "You can be like God." Now that would be something to brag about—but it was all lies. And we can fall for the same ones today. Life still turns inside out when false principles of significance are embraced.

Do You Really Want a Storybook Life?

There are so many false places of significance where we can be lured and lulled into thinking we are attaining some real signifi-cance. After all, women are almost trained to look in the wrong places. For example, let's look at some of the common storybook characters many of us grew up on. There is the sweet naïve Sleeping Beauty, who has to wait for a prince to come along and kiss her in order to wake up and be free to live. Little Red Riding Hood, the poor thing, just couldn't follow directions about not going through the forest and gets eaten by a wolf, and a wood-chopper has to kill the wolf and free Red Riding Hood and granny. Rapunzel at least took her destiny in her own hands and decided she wasn't going to be locked in a tower anymore, but she had to use her gorgeous good looks (her hair) as the means to gain a new life. And then there's Goldilocks. She is a picture of women today, flitting from thing to thing to thing, looking for something that will make her life "just right." Like Goldilocks, we are looking for significance in all the wrong places.

It Feels So Good

Kristie was smart, talented and had a bright future ahead of her. On and off she'd struggled with her self-esteem, but no one in her church expected her to give up all of her hopes, dreams and scholarship opportunities for a guy. She said her slide into the relationship began slowly; Jim was "just a friend." He was older, he had children by another woman, and he seemed confused, mixed up. Kristie thought she could help. But then Jim began to tell her all the things she longed to hear: *You're so beautiful. You are so sexy. I love your hair, your eyes, your smile...* Kristie began to drop her other friendships to spend more time with Jim. It was as though she was addicted to his compliments.

Her family and friends tried to throw up warning flags. Dad pointed out Jim couldn't keep a job. Mom pointed out that he wasn't a Christian. Her sister pointed out Kristie drove him every-where and paid for the dates—"He's using you!" Her friends tried to invite her to their activities because they all saw her isolating herself from her schoolwork, her musical talent and her future college and career plans. Kristie ignored all the warnings. She had wanted to wait until marriage to give away her sexuality but when

Jim whispered in her ear how much he wanted her, she gave in. She was quite surprised by how easily she gave up something she thought she had valued so much. She rationalized in her head even during the act, *But he loves me. I know he loves me. I know he wants to marry me.* Soon Kristie didn't feel like going to church. "Those people are so hypocritical. No one is really walking the walk." Kristie would roll over and dream of Jim. Her friends would call her and say they missed her. Kristie responded, "Everyone is just so immature at youth group. They just aren't at the place I am. They are so juvenile—like kids."

Kristie gave up her scholarship that fall. After all, she rationalized, *Jim will marry me soon. I know he will.* But he didn't. He kept promising Kristie, "Soon, it'll be after I get a job." Then it was, "after I get visiting rights to my kids." Then it was "Kristie, you don't own me. Quit asking me! I'll marry you when I'm ready!" All the while Kristie was giving herself sexually to Jim. The compliments became fewer and fewer, yet she still hung on to each word when they came. Finally, five years later, Jim married Kristie. "If it means something to you fine, we'll get married," he huffed. On the honeymoon, Jim preferred football and the adult movie channel over spending time with Kristie.

"I felt so ashamed. I didn't tell anyone. Not my sister or parents. They'd tried to tell me Jim wasn't good for me, but I didn't listen. Now I was ashamed."

Kristie soon found herself pregnant. "Fine Kristie, but don't expect me to help with the kid," Jim announced. Suddenly, Kristie understood why Jim hadn't received visitation rights for his other kids. She wondered if the money she'd given Jim for child support ever even went to the children. She called his ex-wife and she cried into the phone, "No, no, I haven't received a dime from him. He doesn't give a damn about anything or anyone except himself." Kristie looked down at her swollen tummy, and tears brimmed to the surface. Jim came home from his regular nightly stop at the neighborhood bar. "You're getting too fat!" he exclaimed as he walked in the door.

Kristie confronted Jim, "What happened to all the money I gave you for child support? I just talked to your ex and she hasn't ever received anything from you!"

Jim walked over and slapped Kristie. "Don't you ever check up on me! What does it matter where I spent the money? As ugly as you look, I should go spend it on a whore." Kristie, holding her blackened eye, tears streaming down her face, wondered if he already had. Suddenly her whole world crashed at her feet. *I'm 26. I'm in a dead-end job and married to a man who hits me, who doesn't have a consistent job and who spends my money on the other women he sleeps with. He used to make me feel so special, so important, so significant, but now I feel like I'm not worth anything and I'll never go anywhere in life.*

There are millions of Kristies in the world. Maybe you feel like Kristie or have in the past. Because my husband, Bill, and I also write marriage books, I work with many women who have lived lives like Kristie. Sometimes they get tired of being beaten, sometimes they fear for the lives of their children, sometimes they are tossed aside for a younger woman or left by an already irresponsible husband as he steps out of their life in search of the next party. What amazes me is that all the women that come to see me have the same opportunity to change their life, to start over again. I explain the processes we must walk women through in order to rebuild their lives, but only about half decide to go the distance and allow God to remake their sense of significance. The others simply meet another guy, usually while they are out dancing or at a bar, and they sleep with him and start the same bad cycle all over again.

I've seen bright, articulate women go from man to man to man, dragging their children along with them through all the relationships because they have bought the lie that a man will make them feel significant.

Without some structured help the cycle won't stop. Only a direct intervention from heaven will reach down and break the destructive pattern. Only unconditional love from the Father will take your battered heart, bandage it up and give you a new identity and a source for significance that will replenish rather than drain you. It can be hard work to allow God to rebuild your sense of significance. But it is harder work to not allow Him to rebuild your life—it just doesn't feel like it at first!

If you are single, complete the chart on page 29 as a safeguard to keeping your significance coming from your relationship with God rather than from any man. Make a list in the first column of traits you'd like in a future spouse (this is how God would treat you!); then write down how you will know the man has the trait, and finally write down clues so you'll know if he does *not* have the trait. This will serve as a grid so you can logically think through any future relationships. For example: In the attributes column I might have: *Respects women.* In the green-light column: *He listens to me when I talk, he respects my personal boundaries and physical standards, and he is a gentleman with polite behavior.* In the red-light column (which means address these if they come up and run the other way if there is little change or too many red lights): *It might be the way he talks about his mother. He doesn't keep his promises.*

Anna was a woman who understood the importance of recognizing a quality man when she saw one. She was widowed early, then spent most of her best years of life serving in the temple. The Bible explains that, "she had lived with her husband seven years after her marriage, and then was a widow until she was eighty-four. She never left the temple but worshiped night and day, fasting and praying." She was a behind-the-scenes kind of woman, but she took advantage of her time among the priests. Anna learned all about the Messiah, who was expected to arrive on the scene anyday. When she saw Mary and Joseph, with the

How Can I Decide?

Attributes	Green Light	Red Light
Character traits I want in the person I marry someday.	How can I tell the trait is there?	How can I tell the trait is NOT there?

baby Jesus, heading into the temple to dedicate Him, she knew she'd found what she had been looking for. "Coming up to them at that very moment, she gave thanks to God and spoke about the child to all who were looking forward to the redemption of Jerusalem" (Luke 2:34-36).

She was so excited about finding a quality man—the God of the universe in human form—that she told everyone she'd come to know while serving in the temple. Probably the entire community was abuzz with the news. Anna, the woman without a man, was used by God to share the best news that mankind had ever heard.

It Looks So Good

She had no power of her own. She could do absolutely nothing about the state her life was in. Most people would say her prospects for getting ahead were dead. Her options were stone cold. A tailored navy suit couldn't even get her out of this jam. The problem was terminal. Tabitha was dead. Not figuratively, but literally, dead. In a few short verses, we read about a woman with no power who was given God's power—and God used her, in spite of her seemingly powerless state.

> In Joppa there was a disciple named Tabitha (which, when translated, is Dorcas), who was always doing good and helping the poor. About that time she became sick and died, and her body was washed and placed in an upstairs room. Lydda was near Joppa; so when the disciples heard that Peter was in Lydda, they sent two men to him and urged him, "Please come at once!"
>
> Peter went with them, and when he arrived he was taken upstairs to the room. All the widows stood around him, crying and showing him the robes and other clothing that Dorcas had made while she was still with them.

Peter sent them all out of the room; then he got down on his knees and prayed. Turning toward the dead woman, he said, "Tabitha, get up." She opened her eyes, and seeing Peter she sat up. He took her by the hand and helped her to her feet. Then he called the believers and the widows and presented her to them alive. *This became known all over Joppa, and many people believed in the Lord* (Acts 9:36-42, emphasis added).

God's power frees us to be used. Our power binds and blinds our hearts.

Power

Power is so subtle as it weaves a web around your heart. Power can begin with such good intentions. A job promotion, a new career opportunity, a new business adventure, the thrill of owning your own company are all very good things which can also become a very deceptive trap of false significance. It is so easy to become accustomed to external rewards that internal rewards pale in significance. The name plate, the business award, the company perks become more important than that still, small voice wooing you to Himself.

No godly woman ever sets out to put career ahead of a husband, a child, a ministry—or ahead of God. It happens so gradually that it would be like watching grass grow or a kettle boil. The change can be hard to discern—but usually you sense the change. Things you previously wouldn't have accepted you now rationalize as okay, necessary or even good.

Several years ago, a woman, Gina, came to me. She was worried about her three daughters. One was out of the house, living with a boyfriend, the next two were 15 and 13, and she was concerned about their grades, choices of friends, and so on. I asked her about their lives, then her own. I found out that she was gone from the house from 6 A.M. until 7 or 8 P.M. every day, as was her husband. Her two youngest daughters were unsupervised from 2:15 until 7 or 8 P.M. I mentioned that they might consider a career shift and suggested tag-team parenting, job sharing and part-time work as possible solutions so the girls could have more direct time with them. I could tell that mom was struggling with the suggestion. I asked her about her job—she talked for 40 minutes about how wonderful it was. She was excited, animated and protective over a very nondescript office job where she worked for a little over minimum wage and had to commute an hour each way to get there. I could tell this job was extremely important to her heart. It seemed to be her entire world.

A few weeks later, I saw the mom at church and she said they had decided to "just see what happened" with the girls. Again, I suggested that it only takes a very small amount of time to change the course of these young lives and since economically they could swing it, she might reconsider some creative work arrangements—maybe even work from home.

To make a long story painfully short: Over the years I have seen the oldest two daughters become pregnant at young ages and outside of marriage. The third ended up in juvenile hall for a time. Mom continued to work, and eventually she also had an affair and abandoned her husband and family for the other man. I recently saw her. She is in an unhappy marriage, in a job that still eats up all of her time and she looks twice her age. Yes, Gina climbed a couple of rings up the career ladder, but at too high a price. She gained some external significance in a temporal way, but she has never found significance that lasts, the kind that brings hope, peace and joy.

When I began writing from home, I asked God to show me a red flag in each one of my boys that I could pick up on so I would be able to visibly see if they were carrying stress that wasn't theirs. After I prayed, I noticed the red flag with Brock was when he became more distant emotionally. He would always do well, he just would not connect as much emotionally to Bill and me—because time is what opens him up. Zach's red flag is easy to spot—he gets grumpy and sloppy. Stress makes him care less about life. Caleb gets tired and whiney, also an easy red flag to spot. I also began a conscious effort to notice how often I would say to the boys, "Hurry up. We have to go." The more often I said those words, the more likely the boys would be carrying stress from our grown-up world.

How about you? What would happen if all the external rewards at your place of employment were stripped away? Would you still feel positive about your career? Is your working interfering with some of the other things you value in life? If so, how? Brainstorm a list of ways to keep your career in check. How will you know if it is becoming too important to you? Ask God to search your heart to see if too much of your identity and significance is being derived from your career.

Title

What if all your titles were suddenly taken away from you? Make a list of 25 ways to describe yourself—but you can't use the titles wife, mother, or any job or volunteer job titles. It's a tough assignment, isn't it? Most of us think titles aren't that important to us, yet we'd have a difficult time describing ourselves without them.

What if you not only didn't have a title, but the things people called you behind your back weren't positive—would you feel very usable to God?

One woman in the Bible had lived such a checkered past that she not only didn't have a title, she isn't even named in the passage of Scripture that talks about her. If the people of her town were asked to title her role in the community they might choose "streetwalker," "loose woman," maybe even "slut." She had many cultural strikes against her. She was a woman—no teacher instructed women until Jesus broke this mold. She was a Samaritan, a part of a people with apostate half-truth theology. She was sexually impure. She had been married to many men and the man she now lived with was not her husband. But Jesus saw beyond the negative titles all the way to her searching heart.

The woman at the well, the woman with no name and a bad reputation, had a dialogue with the Savior over who is the Living Water. The light went on in her heart and she reacted: "Then, leaving her water jar, the woman went back to the town and said to the people, 'Come, see a man who told me everything I ever did. Could this be the Christ?' They came out of the town and made their way toward him" (John 4:28-30).

In this passage, a woman exchanged her titles, all negative, for a new title: believer in Christ. Everyone in the town probably knew her because she'd lived such a wild life—and maybe even partied it up with some of them! And it was those same relationships of hers God redeemed out of darkness and used to bring people into the light. She was so excited about her new discovery of Christ that she forgot why she had come to the well in the first place! She just ran to tell everyone she could think of the good news—and they came! They followed a woman with no title, absolutely no credibility and no clout, out of the city and to Jesus' side. Does it take a title to earn the ear of a person? No, it takes a changed heart.

Money

Sapphira and her husband were committed to the early church. They helped get it off the ground. But their hearts drifted. They voluntarily joined a community of believers that decided to have everything in common. It was not required, it was a choice. Everyone was selling their personal worldly possessions and putting the money into one account. This couple sold a portion of land, then made a decision that profoundly influenced their future: they held back a portion and *lied about it*. Holding it back wasn't the issue, lying was. When they each walked in and each lied about the land and contribution they were struck dead. I think it was because the church was so young in development, God had to make a point: "You can't serve two masters. It's either money or Me."

The outcome is dramatically different when there is a different attitude about money: "I commend to you our sister Phoebe, a servant of the church in Cenchrea. I ask you to receive her in the Lord in a way worthy of the saints and to give her any help she may need from you, for she has been a great help to many people, including me" (Romans 16:1-2).

Phoebe is called a sister, a servant. She didn't have business cards or a gold name plate on her door. She didn't have riches. There is no mention of her owning a Fortune 500 company. She didn't have a title, material possessions, a house at the beach and a country club card. No, she had something better—Paul's personal recommendation so others would immediately respond to her just as positively as Paul did when he thought of her. She had earned a good name. Proverbs tells us, "A good name is more desirable than great riches; to be esteemed is better than silver or gold" (Proverbs 22:1). A good name is even better than a write-up in *Business Weekly* or the society page. What Phoebe earned was influence. God used her to be "a help to many people." God also used her as an example. She may have been a servant, but she's a well-known servant now because God thought enough of her to include her and her good works in the pages of Scripture.

The contrast between these women is stark. Making money isn't the issue, it's when it grabs your heart and yanks you away from God that there is a problem. One Sunday morning I had the hardest time enjoying the music of our worship service, concentrating on the sermon or praying. Everytime I tried to focus on

Jesus, my mind would hop back to a business venture I had just committed to. It wasn't a passing preoccupation. I was submerged in deep contemplation about how to make a buck! And I hated it. I decided if I was going to be ripped away from Jesus because of the new business opportunity, it wasn't an opportunity at all but an obstacle. I walked away from that particular stumbling block to my faith.

If you lost all your money, how would you feel about yourself? How much money would it take for you to feel secure or complete? Does having money change the way you treat people? Does having money make you feel superior? Having money is a tool. It should be nothing more.

Looks

A psychological study in 1995 found that three minutes spent looking at models in a fashion magazine caused 70 percent of women to feel depressed, guilty and shameful. There are 3 billion women who don't look like super models and only about eight who do.

The average American woman weighs 142 lbs., is 5'4" and wears between a size 12 and 14.[1] Models who twenty years ago weighed 8 percent less than the average woman, today weigh 23 percent less. The average model is 5'9" and weighs in at 110 lbs.[2] It is no wonder that the average woman feels inadequate, and that 1 out of every 4 college-aged women has an eating disorder.

When we take good care of ourselves, that is honoring to God and healthy. But when we obsess about our looks, our size and our fashion IQ, we move from healthy to leaning on our looks for significance. Last year I was watching one of those evening news shows and they were doing a special on eating disorders and successful treatment plans. One woman seemed to have a huge recovery rate because she also addressed the underlying self-image problem in these young women. However, not all of them were pleased. A few were interviewed by the reporter and these women complained that the woman's method of hand-feeding (like a mother bird would feed a baby chick) was too forceful. I know people on the TV can't hear you, but I immediately screamed out, "But you would have been dead if she hadn't! You are criticizing the woman that saved your life!" But that's what happens when we wrap our personhood up in the way we look—our thinking gets affected. Truth no longer seems true.

How about you? Do you think you would be a better person if you wore a smaller size? Would your worth go up if you had more money for fashionable clothes? Does the thought of going out without makeup send chills up your spine? Is your focus on the external shortchanging your internal growth?

This false source of significance sneaks up on our hearts. We all want to look and feel our best. We want that first impression to count. But if we're not careful, our priorities about the way we look can slide right into that number one spot. Dieting is a multimillion-dollar industry. I finally found a diet that has rules I can keep. Rules for this diet are:

1. If you eat something and no one sees you eat it, it has no calories.

2. If you drink a diet soda with a candy bar, the calories in the candy bar are cancelled out by the diet soda.

3. When you eat with someone else, calories don't count if you do not eat more than they do.

4. Foods used for medicinal purposes *never* count, such as hot chocolate, toast and Sara Lee Cheesecake.

5. If you fatten up everyone else around you, then you look thinner.

6. Movie-related foods do not have additional calories because they are part of the entertainment package and not part of one's personal fuel. Examples: Milk Duds, Junior Mints, Red Hots, Tootsie Rolls and buttered popcorn.

7. Cookie pieces contain no calories. The process of breaking causes calorie leakage.

8. Things licked off knives and spoons have no calories if you are in the process of preparing something.

9. Foods that have the same color have the same number of calories. Examples are: spinach and pistachio ice cream, mushrooms and mashed potatoes. Note: Chocolate is a universal color and may be substituted for any other food color.

10. Anything consumed while standing has no calories. This is due to gravity and the density of the caloric mass.

11. Anything consumed from someone else's plate has no calories since the calories rightfully belong to the other person and will cling to his or her plate. (We *all* know how calories like to cling!)

Okay, I'm just kidding! But you laughed because we've all been there. We feel the pressure if we don't measure up to the airbrushed pictures in the magazines—and humor is a way to combat the pain.

I have a question that I've asked myself each day since I was in high school, "Pam, are you spending as much time in the Bible as you are in front of the mirror?" God highlights this priority in 1 Peter 3:3-4: "Your beauty should not come from outward adornment, such as braided hair and the wearing of gold jewelry and fine clothes. Instead, it should be that of your inner self, the unfading beauty of a gentle and quiet spirit, which is of great worth in God's sight."

In each chapter, we'll look in God's Word and let Him tell us who we are. Some powerful verses come right after Peter's encouraging us to cultivate inner beauty: "For this is the way the holy women of the past who put their hope in God used to make themselves beautiful. They were submissive to their own husbands, like Sarah, who obeyed Abraham and called him her master. You are her daughters if you do what is right and do not give way to fear" (1 Peter 3:5-6).

"*You are her daughters.*" The emphasis is on what caused the change rather than the change itself. Literally, the original means "you became her daughters." The way we become daughters of Sarah is through a commitment to developing the habit of doing good and not giving into fear.

But why would we *want* to be daughters of Sarah? The letter of 1 Peter was written to believers who were living in the midst of consistent persecution and difficulty. The goal of the letter is to help believers develop a stable life in the midst of unstable circumstances. The call to submission was for the purpose of simplifying life so they could focus on the priority of salvation. When we are obedient, like Sarah was to Abraham, even when it is difficult to want to obey, God says that act of obedience simplifies our life. When we obey God and focus on the internals over the externals of life, we gain a less complicated life. We become low-maintenance women.

Do you know the difference between low-maintenance women and high-maintenance women? Here are a few principles I have taught my boys so they can steer clear of high-maintenance women:

The less clothes a girl has on is directly proportional to the amount of baggage she is carrying emotionally. Little clothes means many bags. She's a high-maintenance woman. A high-maintenance woman puts people in no-win situations. For example, she'll ask, "Do I look fat in this outfit?" If you say yes, she'll burst out in tears. If you say no, she says, "Oh, you have to say that—you're married to me" or "You're only saying that because I'm your friend."

I'm also giving my boys some pointers on spotting low-main-tenance women because I know marriage to a low-maintenance woman is a lot less complicated and less stressful. I call them LM women:

- An LM woman doesn't ask for compliments, but she graciously receives them when given.

- An LM woman believes *winning* and *whining* are spelled differently and are never used interchangeably.

- An LM woman doesn't try to wear you down, instead she seeks to build you up.

- An LM woman follows as well as she leads.

- An LM woman is more interested in the *team* working than the *theme* working.

- An LM woman knows how to use makeup but she doesn't hide behind it.

- An LM woman believes personal happiness is a benefit, not a goal or right.

- An LM woman accepts men's input without needing their attention.

- An LM woman appreciates her girlfriend's input but doesn't need her approval.

- An LM woman realizes that a bad hair day, a broken nail, a run in the panty hose or a change in plans are a natural part of the ebb and flow of life, not the makings of a tragic epic made for a TV miniseries.

It Sounds So Good

Probably the area that is easiest to rationalize as a true source of significance is your children and your home. Society honors and values us when our kids turn out well. In Christian circles, motherhood is valued, as it should be, but some women value their children and their role as a mother *too* much. This past year, several pastors' wives and directors of women's ministries have shared a dilemma they are experiencing: Mothers are not wanting to attend Bible studies, Sunday School classes or other women's events because they say their children have to come first. The problem is that the reasoning sounds so Biblical, so legitimate.

However, these same mothers are not grounded in their faith. They may love their children, but their significance in life might also be totally wrapped up in their children. When her children are doing well, mom feels great, but if her children stop doing well, she feels like a total failure. Even worse than that, if mom continues to live her life through her children, they will feel pushed, emotionally cramped and may grow to resent her. In addition, tragic results occur in the teen years when mom, having not invested in her relationship with God or in ministry outside her family, lacks the emotional, spiritual and sometimes intellectual strength and information to guide her teens through difficult transitional years.

Sometimes her marriage is even put at risk by this pattern because dad has been out there growing and developing as a person, but mom has been wrapped up with the children. If dad feels neglected he can become vulnerable to an affair.

If we think we cannot live without our children, consider two women whom God honored because they did just that. Hannah longed for a child, waited for a child, prayed and begged God for a child. Hannah vowed to give the child back to God if God would miraculously place the baby in her barren womb. God took her up on the offer. Hannah conceived and bore a son, Samuel, who, when he was just a preschooler, was given back to God. Samuel grew up under Eli's care and became one of Israel's most celebrated faithful priests.

How about Moses' mother? Desperate to save his life from the Pharaoh's killing spree, she hid the babe in a basket and floated him down the Nile to a place where an Egyptian princess drew him out. His sister approached the princess and an arrangement was made to allow the baby to be nursed by an Israelite wet nurse, his own mother. But her time with Moses was short. In Eastern cultures, most children are weaned around five years old, at the latest. What did Moses' mother say to him in those very early formative years to produce a son who would forsake all the power, riches and fame that was within his grasp in Pharoah's household, and instead cause him to choose to align himself with his enslaved people?

I think it is the very act of giving our children back to God that allows us to be a funnel which God can use to grow them. When we hang on too tightly, our children can become possessions of our hearts rather than precious creations in God's hands.

Ask yourself: "Do I use my children as a shield, a way to get out of personal growth activities like Bible studies, ministries, evangelism or volunteer work that would help me discover God or discover the gifts and abilities He's entrusted to me?"

How about your home? Has your home become a showplace rather than a source of ministry? Have you redecorated over and over and over again? Are you spending more time finding just the right antique piece for your living room instead of just the right way to share Christ with your neighbor?

Our homes should be places of order, neat enough to live an organized life, but they should also be places in which anyone would be welcome. How welcome does a toddler feel in your home—or a teen?

Modern women have a tightrope to walk in their search for significance. Many times women will hurl themselves headlong into a career because the career has tangible rewards of money, status and awards. In the process these desperate women rationalize away the needs of their children. In the same way, many women, out of a fear of change or growth, say no to God and use their home or family as a shield from taking God's invitation to grow seriously. Neither one is healthy. Significance can't be found in the externals of life—not career, the perfect home or those wonderful children—significance is only found in a person, Christ.

We don't have to hype ourselves up by depending on a title, material possessions, power or position. You are *strong and honored* (1 Corinthians 4:19). You don't have to grapple or claw to hold on to a symbol of prestige. This is a book about attitudes—most importantly, God's attitude toward you. As you come to believe His opinions about you, it will change your attitudes about yourself. Your foundation is secure. You don't have to go searching for significance—you already have a part in His plan!

Finding the Missing Pieces

Sometimes, God brings someone into your life to give you a glimpse of how your serving Him is significant from His point of view. The more I encourage women to allow God to rework the way they see themselves, the more excited I get about the results. As their own perspective aligns with God's, hope springs—and out of hope, new life. It's as if they find missing pieces to the puzzle of their life.

I asked Lisa, one of the women God brought into my life, to share in her own words the changes that occurred in her life as she allowed God to reshape her view of herself from heaven's point of view. When I first met Lisa, she looked like a model who had just stepped off the pages of a fashion magazine. Her husband was driving an expensive car, her little boy was dressed like a little GQ man. I wondered why her friend JoAnna had said to me in a private whisper as she hugged me, "Meet my friend Lisa. She is really hurting and needs some help." As I spent time with Lisa, I thought of the quote of Mary Kay Ash, "So many women just don't know how great they are. They come to us all vogue outside and vague on the inside." I was privileged to be a part of watching Lisa grab on to the picture God had of her. These are the words from Lisa's heart:

> Once upon a time there was a little girl who used to lay awake in bed at night listening to the sound of her mother and father yelling, arguing and sometimes hitting one another. The little girl would say to herself, *Someday my prince is going to come. He is going to carry me away to a far-away castle and we will live happily ever after.*
>
> That little girl was me. I grew up in a very dysfunctional family. I wanted a fairy-tale life and I thought a prince was my only way to my dream. A prince would come along, rescue me and we would have this wonderful life together. Well, my prince came, or at least I thought he was a prince at first, but he turned into a frog. I thought I was a princess and I had everything I needed in my prince. Imagine my surprise and disappointment when my fairy tale was ripped away.
>
> You see my prince was not a prince. I was in denial. I was living a lie in an unhealthy relationship, striving for perfection, only to receive more abuse from a person who was not connected to God. All my life I have struggled with insecure feelings of not being pretty enough, good enough or smart enough. I strove to feel wanted, loved and accepted and in doing so I set myself up for failure in my relationship with my husband. I truly wanted our relationship to work because, first and foremost, I had made

a commitment to God. However, my husband was not willing to participate. Instead of getting help, he chose to abandon the relationship and sought physical comfort elsewhere.

My fairy-tale life crashed down in tiny pieces around my feet, looking like Cinderella's slipper would have if it had been tossed aside onto the hard pavement. I asked myself, *How did this happen? How could I have mistaken a frog for a prince so easily?* My father was an alcoholic, a drug user and a physical and verbal abuser. I chose my father all over again when I chose my husband. If that's all you know, that's what you attract. But God is so gracious—as I look back, I see how He carried me through some very hard times when I didn't know much about Him.

I remember the feeling of loneliness when my birth mother left and gave me to my father along with my sister and brother to be raised by him. Then I remember my father marrying my stepmother when I was seven. She was my first role model. She was also the first positive influence in my life and I felt, and still do feel, very loved by her. When I was 12, my stepmom could not handle my father's drugs, alcohol and not coming home at nights, so she chose to leave the relationship for her own safety. There I was again, all alone. The one person whom I trusted in, loved and connected with had abandoned me. My sister, whom I was and still am very close to, was in and out of my life as a result of my birth mother wanting her whenever she felt lonely. As I went through the experience of my father's second divorce, I was an emotional wreck. I felt everyone in the world had or would abandon me. I was having a nervous breakdown and I didn't even know it. I went a year and a half stuffing my feelings, not sharing because I was embarrassed, ashamed and unable to trust anyone.

As I moved forward into my sophomore year in high school, I took a creative writing class as part of the graduation curriculum. It was that class that started my recovery process over the divorce of my parents. I had to write a story about something that had happened to me. I chose to write about my parents' divorce and how it had affected me. I will always admire and respect my teacher for encouraging me the way she did. For the first time in my life, I felt I had a gift and that gift was writing. I remember saying to myself after I had written my story, *I'm never going to get a divorce when I marry because I never want my children to experience the pain that I have endured.* Just a short time later, my father was put in prison for smuggling cocaine. Again my sister was sent to live with my birth mother, and my brother was placed in a foster home. I moved out and continued my education. I worked to support myself financially. But there I was again, alone!

There was never a safe environment where I could truly run to and call home. I struggled for years. At age 18 my father died of a drug overdose. I felt all alone again, and even felt responsible for his death. I remember thinking, *If only I could have helped him and got him the proper help he needed.* The truth was that I could do nothing—I was just a young girl. He had made the choice on his own to live out his life in that manner, but I carried this burden in my heart for many years.

At age 24 I married my ex-husband. Little did I realize that I would have to re-live my father all over again. As I look back, God was faithful to me even as I saw my marriage dissolve. God took me out of a verbally and physically abusive relationship and put me in a loving, safe environment by connecting me with friendships that are more precious than silver. After the police had been summoned to my home in a domestic violence call, my friend Debbie came to get me and I stayed with her. I tried to make my marriage work again, but when I no longer felt safe and was afraid for myself and my little boy, she came again and helped me move out of my home to a safe place. I will always appreciate the sacrifices she made for me. God had placed Joanna as my neighbor at that time and she introduced me to Valley Bible Church, which led to meeting Pam and Bill Farrel. Pam and Joanna introduced me to Penny, who would also become a part of my support team. This team counseled me and helped build and restore my personal relationship with God.

During the course of my recovery, I said, _Okay God, if You're really there, I want You to develop me, give me confidence, restore my damaged emotions and show me what Your will is_. One of the first steps of recovery is gathering together a support team of women who all have a strong connection to God. Pam, Penny and Joanna held me accountable, prayed for me, encouraged me and cheered me on through the whole process.

As I began my recovery, I could really feel God's blessings pouring upon me. I developed an undeniable love that I've never known. God just kept answering every request. I was His precious child. I learned we have a gracious and loving God, who is so willing to give us the desires of our heart if we are willing to abide in Him and be obedient to Him. I began a personal relationship with God, going to Him in prayer many times throughout the day.

Many emotions flooded my thoughts when I was going through the recovery process, but I didn't react emotionally. I had made a choice, a decision and a commitment to get help. I did not want to repeat the same relationship over again. I have a son, and I didn't want to subject him to any more pain in his life. I took my son to counseling and I encouraged him to express himself and nurtured his connection to God. I also made sure I was available and present in his life even when it meant putting my own emotions in God's hands while I cared for his needs. As I cared for my son, God allowed me to reflect back on how my own earthly father must have felt as a child. He probably felt the same feelings I went through: loneliness, sadness, anger and isolation. I never knew my grandfather, but from what I've been told he was an abuser too. It's a vicious cycle. Our behaviors get passed down generation after generation. But God gives each of us the option of choosing Him and breaking the cycle.

One of my first assignments from Pastor Bill was to write about my life. I had lost my desire to write when my ex-husband took my journals without my consent and read them and interpreted them into what he wanted them to read. I have to admit that I was somewhat nervous and excited when I was asked to write my story. I remember sitting on my sofa and before I knew it four hours had passed. I felt so alive, so rejuvenated. My passion was back. The gift that God had given me was alive and I felt thankful to be experiencing that desire again.

As a part of the support-group homework, Pam had me choose verses about God and about how God saw me. I began to experience hope again. With the hope grew a desire for a life change. The group had me write down my goals, dreams and desires. I started charting my journey, asking God to lead me all the way. I hung my goals and desires on my refrigerator and bathroom mirror, as well as placing them in my Daytimer. Here were some of my personal goals:

1. Restore my damaged emotions
2. Read Bible daily/prayer
3. Job/more income
4. Money to pay taxes
5. Take vacation with Taylor
6. Start saving for new home
7. Spend more time with Taylor—reading, music, fun things
8. New car

God has provided each and every one. Every single goal has been met. One of the verses that I used to have hanging in my apartment was one that I cling to to this day. Mark 11:24: "Therefore, I tell you, whatever you ask for in prayer, believe that you have received it, and it will be yours."

God used my circumstances to show me other women who were in far worse situations than I had been. I remember talking to a woman who was literally in hiding, in fear of her life with two babies. My heart went out to her. I remember saying, *Oh God, how can I help?* At that moment, God put the desire in my heart to start a ministry for single moms. When I consulted with Pam, I found out that she had been praying for years for a woman who wanted to reach out to single mothers. I began to see myself as a woman God could use. God was pulling the pieces of my life together. I then stepped out and allowed God to use me, my heart and what He had done in my life to encourage other women.

As God continued to rework the way I thought about myself, Him and life in general, I felt courageous, strong and positive. I wasn't just dreaming about being a princess—God was showing me I was a daughter of the King of kings. One day I wrote in my journal to God: *God, You know my heart, You know my desires. In Your timing, when You feel I am ready for a relationship, one of my* requests is that I not be subjected to unhealthy men. Another request is that when You choose to put a good, solid Christian man in my life, here is a list of qualities and characteristics that I would like to be in that relationship:

1. A man who loves You first before me or anything.
2. Someone who loves Taylor as if he were his own.
3. An excellent communicator.
4. Someone with a sense of humor.
5. Someone sensitive, loving and caring.
6. A support person who will encourage me in my desires to write and to minister.
7. Someone who will be a good provider.
8. Gee, God, it would be nice if he sang or played an instrument of some sort.

The evening on the day I penned those words in my journal, I was invited to a customer's husband's fiftieth birthday party. I almost didn't make it there because I couldn't find it, but I eventually arrived about an hour late. I almost turned around but a voice inside me kept saying, *Go—you never get out, Lisa. Besides, what was so unsafe about a fiftieth birthday party? This is where I want you to be.* Little did I know that this would be the night that I would run into my future husband. I had known John for three years, but we had a business relationship. We both had a rule that we didn't date customers or vendors. Well, John had left the company he was with and was moving to Arizona to accept another position with a different company. At the end of the evening, he asked me out. I said, "Sure, give me a call and we'll set something up."

This was perfect in my mind because he was geographically undesirable. In addition, he wasn't my type. You know, the "prince-type" I had always gone for before: arrogant, suave, tall, blond hair, blue eyes, perfect-body type of guy. Then I remembered, *Lisa, you have been attracted to prince-types before—but they turned out to be frogs. Give this guy a chance, he might have character and be a son of the real Prince of Peace!*

Then I remembered the verse I had posted everywhere during my recovery: "It is better to take refuge in the LORD than to trust in man. It is better to take refuge in the LORD than to trust in princes" (Psalms 118:8-9).

I would have missed John if God hadn't remade my thinking in the months before. No, John wasn't the fairy-tale kind of guy I'd gone for before, but he did meet all the things in my letter to God—so much so that he sang in a choir growing up as a child and he plays the clarinet to this day!

One day during this time, a girlfriend and I were talking and she asked me, "If you were to ever get married again, how would you do it?"

Well, being the dreamer that I am I said to her, "I love yellow. I want to get married in Hawaii, the girls wearing yellow chiffon dresses, barefoot, with French manicures and hakuleis around their ankles." I simply set the dream aside, concentrating on the more important issues now before me. I didn't want to repeat a dysfunctional relationship, so before John and I became serious we really took the time to get to know one another. I wanted to make sure that this person was a good, solid Christian man, so one of the first things I did was introduce him to my support team. I wanted any man in my life to pass the test of my friends and their husbands. A safety net under my life was when God showed me the value of surrounding myself with a circle of friends—including those solid in their marriages. Everyone in my world loved John, including my son, so we began some extensive premarital counseling before making a commitment. We also decided that our dating life would be run by God's standards and we committed to not have a sexual relationship prior to our wedding night.

Life is better than a fairy tale. That June, John and I stood in a little green church, called Waioli Hui'ia Church in Hanalei, Kauai. Pam and Bill and many of my support team were there as John and I became husband and wife. The girls wore beautiful yellow chiffon dresses, barefoot with hakuleis around their ankles and necks. The ceremony was a celebration to God and filled with music, the personal vows we wrote for one another and the commitment of love for a lifetime.

The morning after our wedding, we sat in silence, holding each other. In the distance we could see the ocean with waves crashing slowly against the sandy coastline. Piercing through the clouds were beams of light from the sun, and off in the distance was a beautiful, colorful rainbow with the most majestic, vibrant colors that I had ever seen. We felt the rainbow was God's way of reminding us that He is always faithful to bless those who are faithful to Him. And the rainbows of God's love continue in our marriage and in our growing family. I often reflect back on what started it all, a whisper of God's love telling me, "Lisa, I know you're struggling right now but trust in Me." I did then, and I do now because He sees me as I was designed to be and He is daily working out plans to give me a future and a hope.

As you get to know God, He will help you get to know yourself and get to know His significant plan for your unique life. The positive result of this method of God's is when our significance is developed in our relationship with Him, we are free to be good moms, good wives, good career people—and our ability to be good in those areas will come because we don't *need* them for our identity. Because we don't *need* them, we can be servants and not think of ourselves so much. Then God can use us.

I think one college-age student put it best. He was talking with his school friends, most of who didn't know God personally. He said, "You are all looking to things outside of your control to give you happiness. You are hoping that the great job, new car, wonderful family will all work out—then you'll be happy. I'm different. My life is wrapped up in God. It doesn't matter if I get all those external things. I'll still be happy because I have God. I could be on a deserted island and still be happy because I'd still have God." This student understands the source of significance. Wrap yourself in the person of God, and everything else pales in comparison.

❊ ❊ ❊

Putting the Pieces Together

What false source of significance are you most vulnerable to embracing? Lisa finally was able to wrap herself in the Prince of Peace, her only true source of significance. What trait of God can you wrap yourself in? One way to find verses to wrap around your heart is to list the setbacks, shortcomings or footholds that may have been in your life. Do you have negative thoughts that plague your thinking and keep you from stepping out into God's place in His plan? List 2-3 areas that keep tripping you up. Write down antonyms (opposites) of those words, and then look up verses to memorize that will help rebuild your life from God's point of view.

For example:

I struggle with:	*God is:*
Anger	*Peace, calm, love*
Fear	*Confidence, strength,*
Wanting titles to affirm my worth	*A King and I'm His daughter*

Now look up verses that contain key words in the "God is" column. (A concordance will help.) Choose several verses that encourage your heart. String them together to form a paragraph or two that you can memorize and reflect on when you feel vulnerable to false sources of significance. For example, if I struggle feeling inadequate, frozen by fear or overwhelmed, I might string together these verses:

> "Praise be to you, O Lord, God of our father Israel, from everlasting to everlasting. Yours, O Lord, is the greatness and the power and the glory and the majesty and the splendor, for everything in heaven and earth is yours. Yours, O Lord, is the kingdom; you are exalted as head over all. Wealth and honor come from you; you are the ruler of all things. In your hands are strength and power to exalt and give strength to all.

> Now, our God, we give you thanks, and praise your glorious name.[3] The Lord is my strength and my shield; my heart trusts in him, and I am helped.[4] He will not let your foot slip.[5] I know whom I have believed, and am convinced that he is able to guard what I have entrusted to him for that day.[6] The one who calls you is faithful and he will do it.[7] For no matter how many promises God has made, they are 'Yes' in Christ."[8]

Then I could personalize the verses and paraphrase them as if God is speaking directly to me:

Praise be to You, O Lord, God of our father Israel, from ever-lasting to everlasting. Yours, O Lord, is the greatness and the power and the glory and the majesty and the splendor, for everything in heaven and earth is Yours. Yours, O Lord, is the kingdom; You are exalted as head over all. Wealth and honor come from You; You are the ruler of all things. In Your hands are strength and power to exalt and give strength to all, even me. Now, our God, I give You thanks, and praise Your glorious name. You, Lord, are my strength and my shield; my heart trusts in You, and I am helped. You will not let my foot slip. I know whom I have believed, and am convinced that You are able to guard what I have entrusted to You for that day. You have called me and You are faithful and You will do it. For no matter how many promises You have made, they are "Yes" in Christ.

3

A Place in the Son

Why am I doing this anyway?

*D*o you ever wonder, after pushing yourself on an all-night project, or after working year in, year out at the same job, or in the middle of some intense schedule, *why am I doing this?* Sometimes it might be honorable: to keep your word, to fulfill a need, to pinch hit for a friend. But sometimes it might be because you've been set up to do it. You've been programmed to stay in a system that isn't working. Our past does affect our future.

I was raised in a teeny, tiny town in Oregon. Athena was a small clean town of less than a hundred people and I was related to many of them. It was just the kind of town that Norman Rockwell might have painted. It was all-American. But even though I grew up in an incredibly loving community, in a home with a beautiful yard and a welcome mat at the door, behind the white picket fence it wasn't always a place of peace and tranquility.

I was the oldest child and from my earliest memories of grade school, I remember thinking I had to be perfect to be accepted and to feel loved. I wanted all my papers to be A+. I wanted to be the best in my dance class and anything less meant I felt like a failure. Once when I was eight years old, I was taking a ballet class with girls much older than myself, mostly high school students. My teacher happened to correct my posture and I ran to the bathroom and locked myself in and it took my mom and the teacher nearly an hour to talk me out. It seems to me I was always in tears because I always felt like a failure—even though I was an obedient little girl and an "A" student. Why would someone so young be so hard on herself?

I think it was because I had an earthly biological father who loved me deeply and often sacrificed greatly for me, especially financially, but who had a pain deep in his heart and he chose to answer that pain with alcohol rather than a relationship with God. Living with my dad was a Dr. Jekyl-Mr. Hyde experience. Dad would lovingly waltz me around the living room, then a short time later he would lash out in anger. Whenever he drank, he would change.

Going Back to Move Forward

As I look back on my life, I can see when the roots of perfectionism were planted. Once when I brought home a report card in seventh grade, it read 100%; 100%; 100%; 100%; 100%;

100%; 99.9%. My dad had been drinking, so "Jack Daniels" said through my dad, "Pam, why isn't that a 100?" I remember wondering if I would ever be good enough to earn his love.

When I was eight, almost nine, the pastor of our small church (which looked like one of those tiny white church banks that kids put quarters in on Sundays) asked my Sunday School class if anyone wanted to learn more about Jesus. I remember thinking, *Okay, we get Christmas because of this guy—yeah, I'll go to the class.* In the class, we learned much about who Jesus is, and we also had an opportunity to gain a place on the quiz team. Now, because I always wanted to achieve, I wanted a place on that team! I could just see myself, like a contestant on "Hollywood Squares," up on that podium, answering those questions. But to gain a spot on the team, I had to memorize Matthew 5, 6 and 7. While reading Matthew, I came across the verse, "If anyone asks, he receives; If you seek, you'll find; If you knock, the door will be opened unto you." I thought, *Does this mean that if I ask You to come into my life, Jesus, that You'll do it?* There, sitting on my bed, I bowed my head and prayed, asking Jesus to come into my life to be my savior, Lord and best friend. I believe He met me there that day.

I felt free and loved unconditionally. The next day was Sunday, and as was tradition, my pastor gave anyone who wanted one an opportunity to come forward for prayer. I was crying. I remember my pastor asking me, "What's wrong, Pam?" (He did a good job of not rolling his eyes because I was always crying!) I answered him, "I am so happy!"

My best friend, Kelly, one day soon after asked me if I had a quiet time. I asked, "What is that?" She explained that everyday we should read our Bible and pray. So I began to do that. Even though my dad's alcoholism increased, my freedom and joy were not diminished because my significance was being piped in from heaven.

However, after several geographic moves, I found myself reading my Bible less and less and finally not much at all. Those old perfectionist thoughts returned and haunted my teen years. I thought, *Maybe if I get straight A's—then I'll feel loved and accepted. Oh, maybe if I win cheerleader, yeah that will make me feel loved and accepted. Oh, it must be a college scholarship, that will make me feel worthwhile. No, it must be if I dated the coolest guy who drove the coolest car, then surely I will feel valuable. If I win homecoming queen, that crown on my head would surely make me feel validated, right?* Then I got all those things and I still felt empty inside! I was looking for love in all the wrong places.

One day I drove home during my freshman year at junior college and found my parents arguing. Because of my dad's drinking problem, this was a common, nearly daily activity. Dad would rage, Mom would try to calm him down. It was late in the evening, so I turned to my younger sister and brother and said, "I don't know about you, but I'm kind of tired of this. Do you want to go for a drive?" On the drive I added, "I don't remember much from Sunday School, but it seems like we should pray for Mom and Dad." We parked in the middle of a cornfield and prayed for our parents. Now, I'm not sure what I expected. Did I think that because I prayed somehow Ozzie and Harriet were going to come down from TV land and be our parents? Despite my hopes, as we entered the house we could still hear our parents arguing. Because this was so normal and it was almost midnight at this point, my brother, sister and myself went to bed.

About 3 A.M., we were awakened from a deep sleep to the sound of my mother screaming, "Help me! Help me! Someone please help me!" The three of us bolted from our beds looking for her. I know I was thinking, *Oh no! Dad's anger has escalated into violence and Mom needs rescued.* We ran through the dark house but couldn't find Mom anywhere. We pushed open closed doors and still no Mom. We could just hear her scream, "Help me! Help me! Someone please help me!" Finally, Bret, my six-foot brother, bolted through the door to the garage. There was my mom, not in need of rescue, and my dad, who was trying to hang himself with a rope from the rafters. My brother pulled him inside.

I pushed my dad onto the sofa and I knelt on his chest. I turned to my mother, brother and sister and said, "I think Dad really needs us to pray now!" We began to pray. Dad calmed just a little but was still very agitated. I remember thinking, *He looks wild, crazy.* I was scared and trembling. Then I remembered the Sunday School story about Saul. When he was upset David would play the harp and it would calm Saul, so I decided we needed to sing. So we sang every Sunday School song we could think of: "Jesus Loves the Little Children," "Jesus Loves Me This I Know," "The B-I-B-L-E," "I Will Make You Fishers of Men." If it came from church, we sang it. Dad calmed a bit more, but he was still quite upset. Finally, I remembered Dad telling us stories of times when he was a kid that he used to go to tent revival meetings while on a combine harvest crew, sometimes to poke fun of the preachers, but he did say he liked the song "Amazing Grace." So we sang that over and over and over again until the sun finally rose and Dad passed out.

My mom, brother and sister were exhausted—as was I. They headed for bed but I had diving practice at college. I was hoping to find peace and solace in the water. I went to practice and didn't tell anyone what had happened at my house the night before. Then I drove back home, hoping upon hope that I would walk into a house and see the family gathered and they would say, "We can't live like this anymore." But as I walked in I realized my family really didn't want to talk about it—especially my dad, a very successful businessman, who was sitting at the kitchen table, doing his paperwork.

A Change in the System

Nothing had changed in my family that day, but something had changed in me. On that same drive home, God began talking to my heart—not audibly, but my heart heard the message clearly, "Pam, you have been treating Me like I'm like your earthly father, that I'm somehow distant, demanding, unrelenting—but I'm not like that! Dust off that Bible. Get to know Me."

So I began to read my Bible again. Soon after my father's suicide attempt, I read in Romans 8:15: "For you did not receive a spirit that makes you a slave again to fear, but you received the Spirit of sonship. And by him we cry, 'Abba, Father.'" I soon found out that as our children say "da-da" when they learn to speak, Jewish children say "Abba-abba." I realized I had a daddy God in heaven who loved me, not for what I could do but simply because He made me. For the next few years, I began to write down every-time I learned something about God being my father.

As I spent time getting to know God, my freedom returned. Being driven to achieve didn't seem as critical for gaining acceptance, love or significance. Rather, as I felt loved by God, I felt free to be me. In having Him lead me, I excelled—it seemed without much effort. I studied hard, I always fulfilled my promises, but not because I was frantically stressing out to do so. Instead it just seemed the natural thing to do. Achievement started to become a result, a by-product, rather than fuel for the fire of some desperate search for validation.

Steps to Freedom

My heavenly Father loved me too much to not complete His work in my life. Philippians 1:6 says, "He who began a good work will carry it on to completion." One day in a quiet time, I remember God asking me, *Will you look at your dad through My eyes instead of yours?* See, to me, my dad was a no-good alcoholic, but God pointed out to me that Dad was a man separated from God, and that a symptom of that separation was alcoholism. In looking at my dad in this way, I could distance myself from the tentacles of alcohol's negative messages to me. I began to be able to love Dad again, unconditionally, not because he did things to deserve my love (because he didn't very often) but because he was created by God.

I was freed to learn what healthy love looked like. I had been chasing love, filling my life with men and often dating many at the same time. I wanted to wait until marriage to enjoy my sexuality but before this point I had been running out of reasons to wait, so pressure from my boyfriend at the time was mounting. As I was freed to love by God, I was also freed from the pressure of feeling I had to give away my sexuality in order to gain love. I broke off a relationship that was not honoring God. Also, I quit dating for six months because I wanted to see if I could exist without the identity of being someone's girlfriend. I found out that not only could I exist without dating, I could choose to have standards for those men I would someday date. As God rebuilt my view of myself from His point of view, I gained the bonus of having Him rebuild my view of love, romance and marriage.

God continued to remake the warped way my mind thought over the next year. As I looked in my closet one afternoon in my dorm, I thought, *Hmm, I have a date next Friday. I need a new dress, new shoes and maybe a new trench coat—I think I'll go see Dad.* My dad had a habit when he would drink. He would do or say something hurtful, but then the next day he wouldn't really remember much of what happened (an alcoholic black out), although he would vaguely remember feeling bad about what had transpired. When he felt bad, he would open up his wallet and pull out some cash or a credit card and try to buy us off, thus easing his conscience. I headed up to visit my dad, knowing full well he'd drink, knowing he'd feel bad, knowing he'd give me money—and thus

I could buy a new outfit. I had begun to plan my life around my dad's guilt.

On that four-hour car trip to Dad's place, God got my attention. *Pam, do you want to be the kind of woman that manipulates people based upon their pain and guilt?*

No, Lord.

That day I gave up my right to manipulate my dad based on his guilt. This was a *big change.* You see, a few years later Bill and I dated and became engaged. A few days after our engagement, my father, who traveled as a part of his job, was in town and wanted to take Bill and me to dinner. It was a nice dinner. Dad was on his best behavior, he was dressed in a suit, he was sober and he was actually listening to Bill and me in conversation. Then he said, "Kids, why don't you two come up to Stockton and see me in a few weeks. I'd like to give you some money for the wedding." He named an amount.

A few weeks later, hopeful that this too would be a positive trip to my dad's, Bill and I headed up to Stockton. When we arrived at Dad's house, he wasn't there. He had been out water-skiing with his buddies. When Dad water-skies, Dad drinks beer. When Dad drinks beer, he gets in a "barbecue" kind of mood. Shortly after he arrived, he threw some meat on the barbecue and continued drinking. Well, when you drink that much beer, what you get when you barbecue is a burnt offering. Dad plopped this unknown meat source onto a plate and when the fork wouldn't even go in, we realized that no one could eat it.

I said, "That's okay, Dad. I didn't come to eat your meat. I came to spend time with you. I'll just order some pizza." The pizza arrived and we sat down at the dining room table. Because my dad had been drinking beer all day, when he sat down, he lost his "cookies" all over the pizza. I remember throwing myself across my new fiancé trying to spare him from the scene, as if I could do that! I got my dad cleaned up and packed off to bed. I cleaned up the kitchen, then said to Bill, "We need to go to the park and pray. I can tell you that in the morning Dad is going to feel really bad about what has happened. He may not remember exactly what he's done, but he will feel bad. We need to decide right now how much money we would have taken if he would have been sober because I don't want these strings of guilt to follow us into our new relationship." As we talked and prayed, we remembered the amount Dad had offered to give us at dinner weeks before when he was sober and we decided that we would accept no more than that amount.

Sure enough, the next day Dad woke up feeling really bad. He offered to write a check that could have created a "Princess Diana" wedding for me. But I knew I didn't want my significance to be built on a false foundation. I would rather have a simple wedding with a pure heart than a fancy one with strings.

Step by step, God was asking me: *Will you forgive your dad? Trust Me, as you forgive, you will gain freedom.* I forgave and as I did, I gained freedom to move away from false significance and towards the true significance given by God. God is in the process of remaking me.

Wounded Healers

Bill and I have enjoyed the benefit of having Jim and Sally Conway as wonderful mentors in the faith and in ministry. Jim once told Bill, "We are all wounded healers." I have seen that is true. The more I allow God to redeem my darkside, the more freedom I experience, the more I am free to be used by God. Sam Rima and Gary McIntosh, in their book *Overcoming the Dark Side of Leadership,* describe the importance of allowing God to redeem back the hurts and rebuild our lives with His love:

> It was during this research that it became clear that a paradox of sorts existed in the lives of most of the leaders

who had experienced significant failures: The personal insecurities, feelings of inferiority, and need for parental approval (among other dysfunctions) that compelled these people to become successful leaders were very often the same issues that precipitated their failure.[1]

It seems God takes our God-given personality and giftedness and, if we are willing, redeems back our inferiorities, mistakes and hurts to shape us into the people He wants us to be.

Most often their ambition has been a subtle and dangerous combination of their own dysfunctional personal needs and a certain measure of their altruistic desire to expand the kingdom of God. However, because ambition is so easily disguised in Christian circles and couched in spiritual language (the need to fulfill the Great commission and expand the church), the dysfunctions that drive Christian leaders often go undetected and unchallenged until it is too late.[2]

So You're Not Perfect!

I believe God gives us opportunities to deal with these dysfunctional foundations of significance if we are aware of them. If I embrace my imperfections, I can be free to be a woman God can use. When I did my quiet times of all the "You Ares" that God says about us, I was very encouraged by all the positive ones like: you are strong, chosen, children of the promise, standing firm and so on. But for me personally, the ones that were most freeing were the ones that at first appeared negative. Some of these I didn't like and I wished they weren't even there! For example, 1 Corinthians 3:2-4 explains "you are still not ready. You are still worldly." Romans 6:19 says, "You are weak in your natural selves." Hebrews 5:11 mentions that we are "slow to learn."

I came to realize that freedom isn't the same as denial. I am slow to learn, I am weak, I am still worldly, and if I ever think I have arrived, I will be lying to myself. These things are just as true about me—and you—as all the other more positive things God says about who we are. Jesus has done us a favor when He tells us in Matthew 15:19: "For out of the heart proceed evil thoughts, murders, adulteries, fornications, thefts, false witness, blasphemies" (NKJV). It is to our advantage to know that we have a bent towards selfishly wanting our way over God's way. And every time we give into our selfishness we prove: "There is no one righteous, not even one; there is no one who understands, no one who seeks God. All have turned away, they have together become worthless; there is no one who does good, not even one" (Romans 3:10-12).

Consider how this dark side becomes apparent in real life. I received some quotes that were said to have been taken from federal employee performance evaluations. Ask yourself if you've ever felt like these were true of you:

> Since my last report, she has reached rock bottom and has started to dig.
>
> When she opens her mouth, it seems that this is only to change whichever foot was previously in there.
>
> This young lady has delusions of adequacy.
>
> This employee should go far, and the sooner she starts, the better.
>
> Not the sharpest knife in the drawer.
>
> Bright as Alaska in December.
>
> One-celled organisms out-score her in IQ tests.
>
> Has two brains; one is lost and the other is out looking for it.
>
> She's so dense, light bends around her.

If you give her a penny for her thoughts, you'd get change.

Takes her $1\frac{1}{2}$ hours to watch "60 Minutes."

Got a full 6-pack, but lacks the plastic thingy to hold it all together. (My personal favorite!)

God knows that we don't always have it all together. But it is also clear that as we embrace our imperfections and acknowledge that we are weak, then we gain the ability to become strong. Paul said: "When I am weak, then I am strong" (2 Corinthians 12:10). Yes, we are still worldly—babes—carnal—but we can choose to change this state and become spiritual. But Romans 3:23 is clear, "all have sinned and fall short." We are all imperfect and are weak in our natural selves.

We are weak, but He has made us strong. How? How does this transformation take place? Romans 3:24 says that we "are justified freely by his grace." Justification is a legal term. It is a picture of all our sins being logged into a portfolio or file. (And each of us has a thick file of imperfections, mistakes and sins! Think of it as your permanent record or, as those in law enforcement call it, your jacket.) Then God sent his Son, Jesus, down to earth to live a sinless life. He had a file folder full of perfect credits, He is righteous. On the cross, God took our sins from our file and switched them with Jesus' righteousness. Jesus paid the penalty for our file folders—for our jackets of imperfections! God now looks down on us from heaven and sees Christ's righteousness where our sins once were.

Justification is a one-time act that happens when we meet Christ. Having justified us, God begins a process of sanctification. Second Corinthians 3:17-18 tells us: "Now the Lord is the Spirit, and where the Spirit of the Lord is, there is freedom. And we, who with unveiled faces all reflect the Lord's glory, are being transformed into his likeness with ever-increasing glory, which comes from the Lord, who is the Spirit." So Jesus is in the process of moving us from the weakness that characterized our lives before conversion up towards our position of strength as seen from heaven. He's renewing and rebuilding us. It is only as we continue to acknowledge our imperfections that He transforms them. I love the prayer in Psalm 139:23-24:

> Search me, O God, and know my heart;
>   test me and know my anxious thoughts.
> See if there is any offensive way in me,
>   and lead me in the way everlasting.

Playing a New CD

After seminary, Bill and I headed to youth ministry. One of the challenges was needing to staff the junior high, high school and college all at the same time on Sunday morning. I volunteered for the junior high. The group quickly grew from a handful to about 70 kids. But as the group grew, being junior highers, they became more and more of a challenge to control—and I do mean *control*. Because that's what I tried to do. Teaching was secondary to keeping them in order. I hated it when those energy-packed kids seemed out of my control. One day I thought I was going to lose it. I felt anger rising to the surface and it was going to erupt like Mt. Vesuvius all over those kids.

So I prayed! *Help me, Jesus.* And He did! That day, I realized, they were just being junior highers and it was *my* problem, not theirs, that God wanted to work on. I was a control freak—I had seen it in a variety of smaller issues in my life and relationships. I knew that because I had grown up in a home that was out of control, I could easily become a controller! I had to replace the old CD message that programmed me with a need to control with a new CD that reminded me that only God is in control. Instead of seeking control, I asked God to begin redeeming part of my personality.

The first step was to forgive my dad for producing this trait. As I forgave and yielded, I experienced growth. God is every day working to whittle down the control freak in me!

This same anger has another ugly head. It used to be that when stress or strenuous circumstances hit my life, anger was the first emotion that rose to the surface. Often, this anger would be taken out on Bill, undeservedly so. One day as I was ranting, Bill walked over, wrapped his arms around me (he had to or my flailing arms could have hurt him!) and he said, "Pam, what are you really feeling? Are you really this angry with me or could it be something deeper?" He was right, I had a deep-seated fear of failure! Again, I forgave Dad for planting the seed and asked God to redeem it. Now when I am feeling that same stress and anger rising to the surface, I ask God to help me communicate my insecurities rather than get angry. I will say something similar to, "Hey, I need to share something with you. I'm feeling like I might fail here. So I have some strong emotions inside. Can we stop and pray, then brainstorm a way to alleviate this fear?" Now there are rarely the hysterics, fireworks and rantings that I experienced years ago. I am freer every day as a new CD plays in my heart and head.

Bill and I have experienced much freedom in forgiveness and we find that we use it in all of our counseling. There are six basic principles, and if a person can walk their way through these six statements, they gain a handle on how to forgive in a tangible way.

Forgiveness says:

1. I forgive _____ (person) for _____ (offense).

2. I admit that what was done was wrong.

3. I do not expect _____ (person) to make up for what he has done.

4. I will not use this offense to define who _____ (person) is.

5. I will not manipulate _____ (person) with the offense.

6. I will not allow the offense to stop my growth.

These are all principles taken from what Jesus did on the cross for us. He knew our sins—each and every one of them—and He died for them. But to receive the benefit of Christ's death on the cross, we have to admit we are wrong. We have to repent. God didn't expect us to make up for our sins. He knew we couldn't—it is impossible. God doesn't define us by our sin, rather He defines us from His point of view. He doesn't manipulate us with all He knows about us. He doesn't allow our imperfections to keep us from Him, He allows us to partner with Him for our growth.

Why am I Doing This?

God knew that I needed to continue to allow Him to redeem my dark side. While spending time with Jim and Sally Conway, Jim told me, "Pam, people who have been wounded, like us, from homes like ours, often make decisions based on our sickness, not health. It is as if you have a tube inside you. You receive a compliment and it feels so good going down. But the bad thing is it is a bottomless tube, so the positive praise goes right out the bottom. We constantly need more praise. We easily fall into the trap of making our decisions based upon what will bring us the most praise, the most public applause, the greatest possibility for compliments. But because the tube is bottomless, it is self-defeating. You can't fill the tube."

I responded back to Jim, "Like Solomon says, vanity of vanities, it is all vanity. No amount of praise will do it, so I need a different standard of decision-making, right?" I knew I had always struggled with pleasing people, even if in doing so I was caused distress. I would always seek to alleviate other's stress—especially when it would result in praise of any kind.

"Right," said Jim, "because our wounds make us vulnerable to praise, we can also be easily manipulated and sell ourselves to anyone or anything, just to get some praise."

"Like selling our birthright for a pot of stew?" I smiled. I knew exactly what Jim was talking about. I had been aware of this "tube" in me for awhile. It was only my quiet times and God daily centering me that kept me from chasing praise with a "get-it-at-all-costs" attitude. My daily time with God kept me reaching out, stepping out in obedience instead of just staying in my safety zone where I would be assured of successes and praise.

In risking I actually receive affirmation because I am growing as a person. But it can be a scary place emotionally, because with each risk there are no guarantees of success or praise. In fact, often in risking people's worlds are shaken up, so criticism is more likely to come your way. I had chosen years before to get off the merry-go-round of trying to please everyone—I knew I couldn't. I had tried and tried to please my dad, and I rarely heard him verbally praise me. I had seen that if I tried to please everyone in ministry, or life, for that matter, I felt like a chicken with her head cut off, frantically running around. Trying to please created a lot of activity but not many results. So I began to ask myself before any decision, "Why am I doing this?" Then I'd run down the checklist: To receive praise? To try to be perfect? To try to control people or circumstances? Are my motives pure on this one? The closer I watch over my motives, the more I am able to enjoy the journey and not worry as much about the outcome. The words of Galatians 6:14 are etched on my heart, "May I never boast except in the cross of our Lord Jesus Christ, through which the world has been crucified to me, and I to the world."

For years, I have trained myself to mentally flip my heart to that page of my mind anytime I receive praise. It catalogs the compliment where it should be, under "C" for Christ. By doing this, I am able to appreciate the person(s) giving the compliment and encouragement and I am able to focus my heart on Christ and all He has done for me. I am also able to carry any kind of responsibility God sends my way because nothing is "too big" or "too small." It's all just a calling. You have yours, I have mine. God can use us when we are not worried about who gets the credit. Anything He asks is a wonderful opportunity—because He is doing the asking.

Overcome Evil With Good

God used one more step with my dad to free my motives and thus free me to make clearer decisions. God kept prodding me to bless my dad. First it started small. I set up all decisions about my dad with one question: What would a loving daughter do in a healthy father-daughter relationship? Then I'd set boundaries to move our relationship towards health (like not talking with Dad late at night when he was drunk but calling him in the morning when he was sober) and I'd have my gestures of love toward him be the same as a loving daughter regardless of how Dad acted toward me. (For example, Dad rarely sent a birthday gift or card, but I always sent him one.)

A few years ago, God began to prod me to write a blessing to my dad. I had learned over the years that my father had never heard the words "I love you" from his own alcoholic father. I learned that he grew up dirt poor, so he also had a huge fear of failure that drove him to workaholism. I never made excuses for Dad, but I did seek to try to understand him and I sought to keep seeing him from God's point of view. A few years ago, at Christmas, I knew it was time to write the blessing. But where do you start when there are so many painful memories and so few good ones? So I prayed. *God, help me write something to Dad so that he will know I love him—but more importantly that You love him. Let him see that Your love can absorb his pain.*

As I wrote the tribute I could see how some of my best traits were ones God had redeemed out of darkness into the light. Because I grew up never knowing when Dad would rage, it was as if I lived my life on alert. Because I've allowed God to redeem that fear, it turned into a God-given ability to read people, to sense how they are feeling. I can read between people's emotional lines. Because I grew up mediating between Dad and everyone in our family, I have the ability to mediate now, which is a handy skill for a leader! But my favorite trait that God redeemed is the one I wrote about in my tribute to Dad.

On Christmas day, I stood and read this tribute face to face to my father:

Our Golden Treasure

It was a sunny Saturday morning. Excited children piled out of cars, baskets in hand. It was the day before Easter, the day of our small town's big egg hunt. I was nervous and excited, as were all the other preschoolers. I held tight to my dad's hand. The whistle blew, and the race to find the prized golden egg was on! I picked up a pink egg, then a green one, and placed them gently in my basket. But what I really wanted was that golden egg. The hunt seemed like it lasted a lifetime. It seemed that no one could find the golden egg.

Dad said, "Come here, honey."

He bent down and whispered into my ear and pointed at the ground. I looked down at a disgusting sight—an egg smashed and broken from being trampled upon by tiny feet.

"But it's broken!" I said to my dad.

"But what color is it, Charlie?" I shrugged my shoulders. "Look close. What color do you see?"

I tried hard to find a piece of shell big enough to discern its color. I picked up a small fragment and yelled, "It's gold! Daddy, it's gold!" But how was I supposed to get it over to the judges?

"Pick it up. Moms and Dads can't touch the prized egg. You have to carry it."

"Ick! It's too yucky, Daddy! I can't."

"If you want the prize, you have to pick it up, but I will help you carry it."

Together we bent down and I scooped up as much of the egg remnant as my tiny hands could carry. It felt awful. Dad slid his hand under mine and together we carried our broken treasure to the judges. I was awarded a huge basket brimming with Easter goodies. Dad was proud of me and I was proud of Dad.

In the years since, I have often thought of that day. It is a picture of our father-daughter relationship. My dad is a lot like that broken golden egg. Dad has often felt inadequate to be all that he wanted to be as a dad. His heart is like that egg—full of prizewinning potential but cracked by the heartache of broken dreams. Dad has a heart of gold but it often goes unseen by those around him. Words fail him. Sometimes his actions fall short of what he'd like to express. But I've always held on to a piece of that prizewinning potential, just like I held on to that small piece of golden shell. I've held on to the golden moments that Dad and I have shared. Like that day in the park, when I was proud of him and he was proud of me. And when times get hard, I sometimes hear that whisper, "…if you want the prize, you have to carry it." So I pick up the pieces of life and carry what life requires me to carry.

No, Dad is not perfect, but neither am I. So I hold tight to that less-than-perfect treasure, because all that has happened—the good and the bad—God has used to make me the woman I've wanted to be. I have become a woman who can look at a bad situation, find the gold in it and go on.

I'm a prizewinner in my Daddy's eyes and his love is a golden treasure to me.

After I read it, tears rolling down his cheeks, Dad said, "Charlie, thanks. Thanks for using your writing to say such nice things about this bad ol', good ol' boy." That was the first time I ever remember Dad complimenting my writing—and the best part was that I didn't *need* it. I could enjoy it, receive it, but I didn't need it. I had already prepared myself to not receive it, so now I could receive it graciously. I wasn't frantic for approval because I had already heard the applause from my heavenly Father. Listen, can you hear it? Your applause is from on high.

❀ ❀ ❀

Putting the Pieces Together

Make a list of some of the negative traits that could have been trained into you while growing up. How could these be affecting your decision-making skills today? Take a step to replace the old CD with a new one. Try one of these activities:

1. Make a list of people and events that you need to forgive and pray your way through the six statements of forgiveness.

2. Pray that God would make you aware of any old CDs that need to be replaced with new messages from His Book.

3. Write a blessing or tribute to someone who has wounded you. In it include how God turned a pain into a positive.

4

A Place of Confidence

Will it ever be good enough?

I love greeting cards. They carry such encouraging messages, especially at Christmas. I post the cards around the archway from my living room to my dining room because they are so beautiful to look at. But however beautiful the card, or however encouraging the message, the card couldn't arrive at my home without the envelope it came in.

It is my habit to pray with the leadership teams at the churches where I speak prior to going to the platform. While in Missouri, one of the women prayed, "Thank you, Lord, for the message Pam is about to deliver to our hearts. Thank you that she is an envelope for Your message of hope and encouragement."

I thought, *Yes! I love it! I am simply an envelope! He is the message; I just have to carry it.*

The more I thought about that analogy, the more I liked it. There are all kinds of envelopes. Some envelopes are bright and colorful like many cute and perky women! Some are professional and functional, like letterhead. Others are more elaborate, the kind of envelope you might pick up at a stationery store for invitations. Other envelopes are very functional manila gals, but these are often entrusted with some important messages. Others of us look like a plain envelope on the outside, but when you open us up, you see we are solid gold like gold leaf foil wedding invitations. Then some of us are like those Airborne Express/FedEx packages—we just do things very, very fast. Just like envelopes, women come in all shapes, colors and sizes, but we are all still envelopes. There is no Envelope Hall of Fame and no envelope IQ test. Every envelope is important because we all carry the message of the hope, freedom, peace and joy found in a personal relationship with God.

Signed, Sealed, Delivered

The apostle Paul explains this role in 2 Corinthians 3:2-3: "You yourselves are our letter, written on our hearts, known and read by everybody. You show that you are a letter from Christ, the result of our ministry, written not with ink but with the Spirit of the Living God, not on tablets of stone but on tablets of human hearts." *You are a letter*.

The phrase "written on our heart" means a past act that has ongoing results. When we decide to surrender our lives to Christ, the Holy Spirit indwells us, sealing us to God.[1] That's when the letter was written on each of our hearts. And because the Spirit wrote the letter, it is permanent, recorded in non-erasable ink.

Everyday, in every way, believers' lives are being read by others. Age isn't a factor in our worth to God, and we've already discussed that size, shape, color and speed aren't factors, either. We're all envelopes carrying a valuable, needed message to the world where we live. We are valuable not because of our outward packaging but because we carry a valuable message. We've been chosen to carry the message of hope.

It's so easy to forget the freedom we have in being God's envelope. One of the things that is a part of my life as a writer is media appearances. Bill and I have our own radio program, but quite often our publishers also have us appear as guests on other radio and TV programs. One year Bill and I were to appear on a national television talk show. As with all television appearances, each guest takes a turn in the makeup chair. This is never my favorite part because since my teen years, I have struggled with acne. I've been under a doctor's care for it since I was sixteen. I once asked a dermatologist, "I'm almost 30, and my face still thinks I'm 17! When will this stop?" He asked some family history questions and said, "Mrs. Farrel, it may never stop. It sounds like it is hereditary in your family." Oh, great news!

I often tease that I have the perfect face for *radio*!

Anyway, I sat down in this makeup artist's chair, and she said as she stared into the mirror, "You don't have a happy face."

"Actually, I am very excited about today. This is a wonderful opportunity." Then I smiled.

"No, you do not have a happy face." Now at this point, I knew she was talking about my skin. She began the usual battery of questions and suggestions all the while reminding me that I didn't have a "happy face." Well, inside I felt the emotions rising, but I didn't want to cry because then I'd have to sit even longer and have my makeup redone! The makeup artist was called by the star of the show into the next room for a brief moment, I looked at my not so "happy" face in the mirror.

Lord, this is really hard to hear. It is doing nothing for my confidence. Please help me get my focus off my not so "happy" face! Okay, God, why did I come? To show my face to those 60 million viewers? No. I have Your message to deliver. This is not about me, it's about You. It's about Your message. Then I looked at my face again. *Lord, I think I look pretty good for an envelope!*

I knew God had chosen me for this task. I was chosen to be His envelope that day. And deliver the message I did!

Return to Sender

Because Jesus chooses whom to send and where, we can be free from some of the insecurities that hold us back. In one of my *Women of Influence* talks, I ask the audience to share what they think holds women back. Everywhere I travel the same few things are mentioned: women feel inadequate; they might not feel smart enough, trained enough or eloquent enough. Women feel they might be rejected. They are afraid that others may say, "Who does she think she is?" or "I don't want to be her friend."

Sometimes we feel totally overwhelmed. We're not sure how we could ever do even one more thing. Thomas Edison said, "Opportunity is missed by most people because it is dressed up in overalls and looks like work." Some of us don't want more work!

A few of us feel men are holding us back. However, most of us believe in the ability of women to find a way to make a difference. Faith Whittlesey said, "Remember Ginger Rogers did everything Fred Astaire did, but she did it backwards and in high heels."

However, the number one, most common fear mentioned is *failure*. We feel like we might step out and fail in front of God and everyone!

Why do we fear failure? In failure, we find the strands of future success. Here are the reflections about failure from people others have called a success:

Medical doctor, Scottish author and social reformer Samuel Smiles said, "It is a mistake to suppose that men succeed through success; they much oftener succeed through failures. Precept, study, advice and example could never have taught them so well as failure has done."

Businessman Thomas J. Watson agrees, "Would you like me to give you a formula for success? It's quite simple, really. Double your rate of failure. You are thinking of failure as the enemy of success. But it isn't at all. You can be discouraged by failure—or you can learn from it. So go ahead and make mistakes. Make all you can. Because, remember, that's where you will find success."

W.E.Gladstone, a four-term Prime Minister of England wrote, "No man ever becomes great or good except through many and great mistakes."

Writer Orison Swett Marden notes, "You cannot measure a man by his failures. You must know what use he makes of them. What did they mean to him? What did he get out of them?"

Joseph Sugarman, a leader in the marketing industry says, "Not many people are willing to give failure a second opportunity. They fail once and it is all over. The bitter pill of failure is often more than most people can handle. If you are willing to accept failure and learn from it, if you are willing to consider failure as a blessing in disguise and bounce back, you have got the essential of harnessing one of the most powerful success forces." H.L. Wayland continues that thought, "Show us a man who never makes a mistake and we will show you a man who never makes anything. The capacity for occasional blundering is inseparable from the capacity to bring things to pass. The only men who are past the danger of making mistakes are the men who sleep at Greenwood [cemetery]."[2]

"If you don't accept failure as a possibility, you don't set high goals, and you don't branch out, you don't try—you don't take the risk," said First Lady Rosalynn Carter.

Politicians grapple with the possibility of eminent failure, and it is that daily face down with failure that propels them into greater leadership. Prime Minister Sir Winston Churchill said, "Success is the ability to go from failure to failure without losing your enthusiasm." Legislator S.I. Hayakawa concurs, "Notice the difference between when a man says to himself, 'I have failed three times' and what happens when he says, 'I'm a failure.'" President Theodore Roosevelt echoes the need for a positive outlook on failure, "Far better it is to dare mighty things, to win glorious triumphs, even though checkered by failure, than to take rank with those poor spirits who neither enjoy much nor suffer much, because they live in the gray twilight that knows not victory nor defeat."

Failure isn't final. Motivational speaker Dennis Witley reminds, "Failure should be our teacher, not our undertaker. Failure is delay, not defeat. It is a temporary detour, not a dead end. Failure is something we can avoid only by saying nothing, doing nothing and being nothing." Film actress Mary Pickford declared, "Failure is not the falling down, but the staying down." Inventor and automobile manufacturer Henry Ford said, "Failure is simply the opportunity to begin again, this time more intelligently."

Warren Bennis, author, educator and sociologist at the University of Southern California, reflects, "The leaders I met, whatever walk of life they were from, whatever institutions they were presiding over, always referred back to the same failure, something that happened to them that was personally difficult, even traumatic, something that made them feel that desperate sense of hitting bottom—a something they thought was almost a necessity. It's as if at that moment the iron entered their soul; that moment created the resilience that leaders need."[3]

Failure does place iron within our soul. Even small failures help mold us into women God can use. In ninth grade, I was ranked number one in the state in gymnastics. I had won all the district and regional meets and all I needed to do was to show up at the state meet, do what I had been doing all year, then I'd win. Things were going well until I rotated to the vaulting event. It was my strongest event. I had a good vault with a higher technical merit than almost every one at the meet. I ran like a steaming locomotive down the runway. I hit the board that was to launch me up and over the vault to a gold medal—instead I heard and felt a CRASH! I had run straight into the vaulting horse. I felt dazed, stunned and the breath was knocked out of me. I heard the crowd hush. I slowly picked myself up off the floor. I was in shock. I had never missed a vault in competition. I rarely missed a vault in practice.

I walked back to the end of the runway, shaking my arms and legs to loosen them up and to regain some composure. My coach gave me a few words of encouragement. I prayed, *Oh, Lord, help me!* I raised my arm high over my head to signal the judges that I was ready, I gave a quick hop and power ran down the blue strip of carpet, intent on making a vault and making it stick. CRASH! I'd done the same exact thing—twice. Not only did I fail once in front of the full gym of spectators, I failed twice! A scratch. No score. My dream of being the state champion was gone.

In that moment, I had to decide how to face failure. Would I run crying from the gym and skip my last event because I couldn't win anyway, or would I rise and act like a champion, even if the gold medal would never hang around my neck? I had already lost once when I failed to make the vault, but if I let my emotions win out, I would lose twice. If I would quit, I'd lose my positive personality, my hope and because I was the team captain, those following me would lose hope too. Blinking back tears, I rose. I bowed to the judges as if I had just landed a perfect 10 vault, then I pulled my shoulders back and marched off the floor to the waiting and welcomed arms of my mother and coach.

I let the tears flow as they embraced me, but then I wiped them away while my coach prepared me for my final event, the floor exercise. I didn't stand on the winners dais that afternoon, instead I was handed a fourth place all around ribbon. Instead of pouting, I chose to shake the hand and hug my teammate who had capture the gold instead of me. She had placed second under me all season, and this was her moment in the sun. My sister, in a lower age division, stood in the first place spot and accepted the roses and the medal. It was a five-hour trip home. I could choose to make everyone miserable with my attitude or I could choose to be happy for my sister. That day I learned that if you act like a champion, even if the outside world doesn't reward your efforts, you still feel like a champion inside.

Educator Edward Dowden said, "Sometimes a noble failure serves the world as faithfully as a distinguished success." How we fail determines our ability to find and stay in our place in God's plan. God's Word reminds us, "Humble yourselves, therefore, under God's mighty hand, that he may lift you up in due time" (1 Peter 5:6).

I believe that it is not the stepping into the place God has for us in His plan that is the challenge. I believe He will be faithful to allow you to hear His voice and answer his call. He cares more about you walking in His will than you do! But the trick is *staying* in that place and tenaciously serving there, no matter the trial. *It's not the getting in—it's the staying in, that is important!* It is easy, when failure comes in like a tornado, to sneak out the back door, to say, "I've survived one storm, I'm not staying around for another!" But if we really believe God's Word, then we are just where God wants us to be when we are humbled by a failure. We are usable, mold-able, listening and ready to be elevated.

Christiana Tsai could have felt like a failure at one time. Born to a vice-governor in a Chinese province, Christiana was educated by Buddhist monks but soon outgrew their knowledge, so she enrolled in a Christian mission school, vowing to never become a Christian. She said, "I made up my mind that I was not going to 'eat' their Christianity so I used to take a Chinese novel with me to chapel…"[4]

Christiana and a friend, Miss Wu, began to write a book denouncing Christianity. However, Christiana began to read the Bible and listen to preaching in English to improve her skills. "God used my love for English to draw me to Himself."[5] Soon Miss Wu also came to faith in Christ. Success, right? Not everyone thought so.

Christiana shared her new faith with her family. She was bit-terly rebuked for disgracing the family name. One brother grabbed her Bible and her hymnbook and tore them to pieces. Her mother was devastated to have a Christian daughter. But Christiana hung in there. She didn't let immediate failure detour her faith. She kept living the life of faith before her friends and family. One by one they slowly responded. Her mother came to faith in Christ and quit a lifelong habit of smoking opium. That change sparked interest in other family members. Mom, two sons and their wives were baptized. Mom opened up her home for Bible studies and at age 62 she learned to read so she could read the Bible for herself.

Christiana began teaching in a government school. During class breaks she talked personally with the students and she opened her home up so that interested students could come and talk about Jesus. Seventy-two of her 200 students came to know Christ. Again, there was outrage. Parents were up in arms! A newspaper article was published claiming the teacher made her students cry, "God! God!" The school's director, Miss Plum, searched the school and confiscated Bibles and threatened expulsion to students caught attending Bible studies. However, the faith of the students withstood the persecution and soon Miss Plum herself came to faith in Christ.

Christiana recorded her journey: "So the brother who tore up my Bible and persecuted me in the early days at last confessed my Lord. In all, fifty-five of my relatives, adults and children, have become God's children...I have never been to college, or theological seminary, and I am not a Bible teacher; I have only been God's "hunting dog." I simply followed at the heels of my Master, and brought to His feet the quarry He sent me after."[6]

Since God is the one choosing us, *when we obey, it will never be a failure—no matter what the results are.* I think we often forget how carefully He chooses and how well He knows us!

He Knows Us

I think J.I. Packer, in his classic bestselling book, *Knowing God*, says it best:

> There is tremendous relief in knowing that His love for me is utterly realistic, based at every point on prior knowledge of the worst about me, so that no discovery can now disillusion Him about me, in a way which I am so often disillusioned about myself....There is, certainly, great cause for humility in the thought that He sees all the twisted things about me that my fellow-men do not see (and I am glad!), and that He sees more corruption in me than that which I see in myself (which, in all conscience, is enough). There is, however, equally great incentive to worship and love God in the thought that, for some unfathomable reason, He wants me as His friend, and desires to be my friend, and has given His Son to die for me in order to realise this purpose. We cannot work these

thoughts out here, but merely mentioning them is enough
to show how much it means to know, not merely that we
know God, but that He knows us.[7]

God knows me. He knows all about me. He knows the good
and the bad. He knows every hair on my head, and every thought
on my mind. He knows my successes and my limitations. He
knows that I am utterly imperfect. He knows yet he still chooses
me. He knows yet he still chooses you. He says: *You are chosen.*

But you are a chosen people, a royal priesthood, a holy
nation, a people belonging to God, that you may declare
the praises of him who called you out of darkness into his
wonderful light. Once you were not a people, but now
you are the people of God; once you had not received
mercy, but now you have received mercy (1 Peter 2:9-10).

His Choosing

When God says we are chosen, He means we are elected—
and He's the only one voting! So when we are all preoccupied
about what other people think and say about us, we are forget-
ting that public opinion doesn't supercede God's appointment.

Not only are you chosen, but you are chosen for royalty. The
connotation of this verse is that we are a part of the King's court,
we dwell in His palace and as a royal priesthood we are given a
share in reigning with Christ. And when we belong to God, we
are preserved for Him and by Him.

Since I am chosen, royal and preserved by God, I trust Him to
be my protection from criticism. I like to picture God as my flack
jacket! As I seek to step into my royal role of "declaring the praises
of Him," I know I will receive some praise and some criticism.
The Bible is very clear that in this world I will have tribulation—
but it is also clear when Jesus says, "I have overcome the world"

(John 16:33). My goal is to grasp what it means to be chosen and royal and God's commitment is the preservation of my person, regardless of the outcome of my position.

Whenever I grasp the understanding of this picture of who God says I am, I am freer to live life the way it was meant to be. From previous chapters, you know that I started out in life not very confident, always wondering if I would ever be good enough to gain acceptance and love. My fears could have grown in intensity over the years until they paralyzed me in life. Many people live lives filled with fears that hold them back from excelling and stepping into their potential.

This last year, my father died. I decided I needed to visit a counselor who specializes in working with those in positions of responsibility and high visibility. He also works well with those who are grieving. Because many people depend on me, I wanted to make sure I worked through my grief in a positive, constructive manner. My counselor gave me a diagnostic test to enumerate the personal strengths and weaknesses of my life. When I got the results back, I was amazed at one of the variables. The test rated a variety of areas, including confidence and a person's ability to see the positive and move forward to achieve positive results in life. The average person usually rates about the thirtieth percentile—I rated 100 percent! Now I think this is a "God thing!" Only God could change a timid little girl who longed for approval into a woman who is confident in her choices and the way she relates to people and life! I believe as I have embraced the fact that I am chosen it has boosted my confidence.

I love the picture in the next part of the verse, "who called you out of darkness, into his wonderful light." Of course I was called out of darkness! Princesses don't live in dark damp hovels. They live and walk in the light. When apathy and lack of integrity are tempting me to cut corners, I am moving back into the shadows and away from the light I was called to. Eighth grader Alberta Lee

Cox wrote, "It's not enough to be good if you have the ability to be better. It's not enough to be very good if you have the ability to be great." When I resign myself to saying *good enough* when I know in my heart that I could realistically do better, I am choosing to go back to living, thinking and acting like I am from the darkness.

When we were in youth ministry, Bill ran a who-can-bring-me-the-biggest-cockroach contest. We had kids bringing us roaches two to four inches long! Each student told a similar story. They had to move quickly to catch their roach because roaches love the dark and the moment you flip on the light they are running for the shadows! We are not roaches. We weren't made for the dark, we were made for the light. If you find yourself more comfortable hanging out with people who love dark rather than light, or if you can't honestly share what you've been doing, watching and reading with other princesses of the light, then be sure you have moved from your place in God's plan.

I sometimes think we ask the wrong questions of ourselves. Instead of asking, "Is this good enough?" and "Can I skate by with this?" we should be asking, "Am I acting like a benevolent princess?" "Am I pursuing God's light in this area?" God has proclaimed we are already "good enough" because we are chosen, royal envelopes! Our job is to take God at His word and act out our position.

We do have a choice because "once you had not received mercy, but now you have received mercy." There must be a point in time when we choose to walk into the light from out of the darkness. There is a moment when we accept His choosing and His appointing us royals. There is a point in time we become envelopes carrying His message of hope.

What is that message? What is that choice?

God's Statement of Love to Us

- **I love you and have a plan for you.**

  "I came to give life—life in all its fullness" (John 10:10).[8]

  "I came so they can have real and eternal life, more and better life than they ever dreamed of" (John 10:10, THE MESSAGE).

  "God loved the world so much that he gave his only Son so that whoever believes in him may not be lost, but have eternal life" (John 3:16).

- **I know you are imperfect so you are separated from My love, and our relationship is broken.**

  "All have sinned and are not good enough for God's glory" (Romans 3:23).

  "We've compiled this long and sorry record as sinners...and proved that we are utterly incapable of living the glorious lives God wills for us...." (Romans 3:23, THE MESSAGE).

  "And when a person knows the right thing to do but does not do it, then he is sinning" (James 4:17).

  "It is your evil that has separated you from your God. Your sins cause him to turn away from you...." (Isaiah 59:2).

- **I love you so I, who am perfect, paid the price for your imperfection so I could restore our relationship.**

  "But Christ died for us while we were still sinners. In this way God shows his great love for us. We have been made right with God by the blood of Christ's death. So through Christ we will surely be saved from God's anger. I mean that while we were God's enemies, God made friends with us through the death of his Son. Surely, now we are

God's friends. God will save us through his Son's life" (Romans 5:8-10).

"Christ had no sin. But God made him become sin. God did this for us so that in Christ we could become right with God" (2 Corinthians 5:21).

"Christ himself died for you. And that one death paid for your sins. He was not guilty, but he died for those who are guilty. He did this to bring you all to God" (1 Peter 3:18).

"The greatest love a person can show is to die for his friends" (John 15:13).

- **To initiate this new relationship, all you need to do is to accept My payment for your imperfection. I cannot make you love Me, that is your choice.**

"I mean that you have been saved by grace because you believe you did not save yourselves. It was a gift from God. You cannot brag that you are saved by the work you have done. God has made us what we are. In Christ Jesus, God made us new people..." (Ephesians 2:8-10).

"If you use your mouth to say, 'Jesus is Lord' and if you believe in your heart God raised Jesus from death, then you will be saved" (Romans 10:9).

"And this is eternal life: that men can know you, the only true God, and that men can know Jesus Christ, the One you sent" (John 17:3).

To accept God's love for you, talk to Him and tell Him that you do. Let Him lead the decision-making part of your life. This is a sample prayer:

Jesus, I am sorry I have chosen to live apart from You. I want You in my life. I accept the payment of love You gave

for me by Your death on the cross. Thank You for being
my best friend and my God.

If you have ever prayed a prayer similar to that one, you stepped into your place in His plan: you are chosen, royal and part of a holy nation. And as a member of the chosen, royal and holy family, your message is the message of the King. That is why you are a letter. You bear the seal of the King. In Bible times, when an edict went out from the king, wax was melted and the king had a signet ring which embossed the wax declaring the message had come from the king himself. That is the picture here. Because you have responded to God's declaration, you bear the mark of the King. Everyone who sees you will know you came from His court. You carry His message. The message, like the one above, carries His love, hope and plan out to others who may not know it yet.

Sometimes we think that because we are bearing God's message the road should be cleared for us. After all, don't the crowds part in the movies when a messenger shouts out, "I have a message from the king!" The crowd then immediately quiets while the messenger reads the king's salutation, and of course they immediately respond in a positive manner, right? Wrong!

A better picture is trying to walk up a crowded down escalator. We keep taking steps forward but the whole escalator is carrying us back down. We talk to the people around us and try to convince them to turn and go up the down escalator with us. At first they think we're crazy, but the more we hang in there and keep taking steps forward, the less crazy it becomes.

That's the picture Jesus gives in the Sermon on the Mount: "Enter through the narrow gate. For wide is the gate and broad is the road that leads to destruction, and many enter through it. But small is the gate and narrow the road that leads to life, and only a few find it" (Matthew 7:13-14).

The whole world is walking toward destruction, but they think it's a party and they don't want to hear any different. In Pass Christian, a small tourist town in Mississippi, Police Chief Jerry Peralta drove up and down the highway, stopping at every door. "Evacuate!" he cried. A hurricane was headed their way. Some listened. Others laughed. At one apartment complex, a large group gathered with kegs of beer for a hurricane party. They'd been through a few hurricanes before and they thought they were kind of fun.

The storm hit at ten that night. A wave three stories high crashed in on the apartment building. The building was torn apart and the dead bodies were spread across Pass Christian. The next day, one little five-year-old boy was found floating on a mattress—the only survivor of the party.

Convincing people of the truth is an upstream battle, an uphill climb and an extreme challenge. All we're asking people to do is make a 180-degree turn around in life!

I think sharing the good news of God's love is difficult for two reasons. One, we are asking them to commit to a person who will turn their world inside out to make it best for them, and change is hard. Two, change in the life of someone we share the gospel with may affect our lifestyle as well. It might involve a big commitment of time or emotional energy. In short, God might change our life in the process of changing theirs. We can become selfish, tentative or reserved because of our own feelings. Here's an excerpt out of my quiet-time journal:

> God,
>
> Who needs more faith? I'm only asking Lupe to make a 100 percent, 180-degree radical commitment. She's living with a condom salesman who is addicted to pornography and he's using her up emotionally. But he pays the bills for her and her three boys (two of which are his).

I know intellectually You promise to be a husband to her and a father to her boys. I know You can provide exceedingly abundantly beyond all she could ask or think. But God, I see a woman with no job skills, no naturally bold nature, no Christian family influence—in fact just the opposite. Sometimes I feel like I'm the only voice of truth in her life at all. Yesterday, she brought me a whole newspaper with New Age articles and products in it. One ad even said You had returned and were residing in some channeler's body! It's just me, asking her to follow You!

She isn't the only one with doubts. I know her life and the lives of those precious children will be so much better with You. I know her eternity would be secure in a relationship with You. But I also know the transition from broken to whole will be painful, time consuming and scary for her—and me. I'm fearing more for my lifestyle change than hers! I already feel tapped out. All my days are filled with needy people. My heart is so heavy already. I'm afraid I'm turning indifferent because of my lack of faith. I lack the faith that You will take care of this needy lost lamb. I've stepped into Your shepherd's shoes and I'm afraid I don't fill them well at all. I need You to shepherd us both!

The word "repent" means to turn around. Go the other way. That is not an easy or popular message at times. As people see us battle against the status quo, they may shake their heads in dismay, they may dismiss us or they may get irritated because we are trying to go up when everyone else is going down. Some will want to follow us, because the message of love, hope and joy is so compelling. But they may be afraid because it looks so hard— but what they don't know is we aren't fighting our way up a down escalator, rather there is an up escalator smack in the middle of the down one! God carries us up. It is not our own strength that carries us up and out with the message, rather God carries us with His strength.

In the example above, I was overwhelmed at the impact sharing Christ with Lupe was having on my own time schedule. I did step out and do an evangelistic Bible study with Lupe. She had more questions still! She was hungry to learn more, hungry to have the kind of relationship Bill and I share, hungry to have her children obey like mine did. She decided to send her son to Christian school before she had made a commitment to Christ. Her son came to know God first. Then her boyfriend was befriended by a pastor on his sales route. (How a condom salesman got connected to a pastor on a friendship level is something only God can do!) Soon I realized there were more than ten strong believers ministering to either her or her family. I wasn't alone. God had answered my selfish prayer of fear even before He answered Lupe's prayers to know Him.

Can You Criticize a Queen?

If we fear for our time, we fear more that we will be criticized. If we're so royal, if we're chosen, then why do we get criticized? If we are an envelope bearing such a great message, how do we handle the criticism that comes our way?

Here's the good news: even Jesus, who was perfect, was criticized! So when we get criticized how do we handle it? Here's the process I go through when I am criticized:

1. Is it valid? The first question I ask myself is, *Do I already know this is true?* There are many times when we know even before criticism hits that it is on its way. We all say stupid things, forget when we should remember, react when we should have not reacted. Sometimes we wish we could just push the rewind button of life!

The most vivid example is from the first year my husband was in youth ministry. The women's ministry at our church was hosting a mother-daughter special event where the daughter wore her mother's wedding gown. (Now this was already skating on thin ice as the girls were wearing them because the moms couldn't fit in the gowns anymore.) The "models" were to be served dinner first so they could change for the program. The men and youth boys were serving the dinner. One of the older women of the church caught my husband's arm, "Bill, If I told you I was one of the models would you serve me first?"

Bill replied without thinking, "Sure, but you'd have a hard time convincing me you were a model." Then it hit him—stupid, stupid, stupid thing to say! He was brand new at the church and he came running over to me to tell me what had happened and get my advice. Well, we both concluded we might have to float a résumé if the woman didn't extend her grace—which to her credit, she did!!

2. Consider the source. There are times when criticism is launched at you and it really isn't about you at all. Because we live in a society where so many people are carrying emotional wounds and baggage, at any time we can set off someone else's issues and not even know it. One day I went to the post office box to get the mail for our organization, *Masterful Living*. As I sorted the mail, I found I had two personal letters. I read the first one. It was a thank you from a woman for speaking at her retreat. The letter said, "What you shared changed my life." Then she went into detail of how it touched her. The second had no return address and it was unsigned. It read, "You can't possibly be a good mother because you were away from your children when you spoke at our retreat." There was no way to talk out with this woman what she meant and because of the postmark, I could tell she didn't know my children or my husband. I had just somehow stepped on an important issue in her life, but because she didn't value me enough to sign it, place a return address or phone number on it, I couldn't give the letter much weight. That day I placed the two letters at the foot of the cross and in prayer said, *God, if there is anything worthy of praise in these letters, I give the praise to You. If there is any merit to any of the criticism, then let specific examples land in my mind. Otherwise, I am going to take every thought captive and plant this criticism in the trash.*

I have found that if I get verbal or written criticism and if it is valid, God has already been bringing it up for discussion in my quiet times.

3. Don't let the squeaky wheel get all your attention. One day many years ago, I walked into my husband's office and found a four-page letter sitting on his desk—all about me! This person had written four pages about what a bad wife, mother, friend, leader—well pretty much I was awful in every area in my life according to this person. I just sat in my husband's chair and cried my eyes out. I cried out to the Lord, *All I've ever done is try to help—and this is what I get?* Then I cried on Bill's shoulder. He replied with sympathetic insight. "Pam, don't let this one person distract you from the good you do for the many."

Over the next few weeks, that advice echoed in my heart again and again. Every time I would think about the letter, I would want to just quit ministry. I wanted to stay in bed, pull up the covers, watch Oprah and eat chocolate—but I didn't. I kept to my mission of encouraging and equipping women.

With this case, I also knew enough about the person to consider the source. The person's home life growing up was close to hell on earth, so I or many other people could have easily set off some emotional trigger.

4. What's there to gain? In this same case, I asked Bill if I should get together with this person and try to talk it out. "I don't think so, Pam. The letter is just ranting. It isn't asking for any solutions or compromises or changes. This person is just raving mad for some unknown reason. No one else feels this way about you or we would have heard about it. What is there to gain? I think all that would happen is that you'd get verbally accosted for an hour or so. You'd feel even worse and you'd have less motivation to help others who need you." I couldn't help but think about Jesus' admonition of "Don't throw your pearls before swine." In some cases, doing nothing but prayer is the best answer.

However, in other cases, when I have asked, "What is there to gain?" I have decided that a work relationship would be strengthened or a friendship deepened if I took the time to listen to a critic and follow up face to face. I especially find this true if the criticism is a small correction or if it is a correction that is repeated from several people who have displayed loyalty to me in the past. In most cases, I simply thank the people for their concerns, then take them straight to Jesus to sort through. By using the process of taking criticism to Jesus, I have much to gain: intimacy with the Savior, perspective from my Creator, and healing of the emotional wound by the great Physician.

5. Bless 'em: The final thing I do when criticism is lobbed my way protects my heart from hardening. It keeps me from cynicism. And it keeps my joy intact. I bless others. After the four-page letter, I sat and wrote thank you's to nearly a hundred people in my church, thanking them for their service, their character and their love. Recently, Bill and I were emotionally blindsided by a criticism that really hurt because the person timed it so it deflated us after a very special, tender and meaningful event in our personal life. I did all the above steps and I was still hurting emotionally. I decided that the best way to recoup my joy was to give, and give sacrificially. I then planned and paid for two weekend getaways for two of our most loyal friends in ministry who have helped us shoulder our load. By blessing others, God blessed me with hope when I was hopeless. The thought of bringing joy to other people's lives helped me focus on their joy rather than my pain.

Jayne grew up in a strong Christian home. She was excited about passing on her legacy of faith to her two sons. As they grew, one embraced the faith and the other rebelled. Her mother's heart was broken when she realized her teenage son had slept with a girl he barely knew and didn't love. A pregnancy resulted from that act. Jayne felt as though her son was critical of all the gifts and sacrifices she and her husband had given him. She felt totally rejected. She struggled with wondering how to relate to this new woman in her son's life, a young woman who had deep emotional scars that had made her bitter, isolated, negative and manipulative. Jayne even struggled with her feelings toward her unborn grandchild. She was hurt and very angry. She was disappointed and disillusioned in her son and life. She prayed, asking God to help her sort through her feelings. *Give me a way to express love, God.* She remembered the verse in Romans 12:21, which says, "Do not be overcome by evil, but overcome evil with good."

Jayne, who is not an especially crafty woman, decided to crochet an afghan for the baby. With each stitch she asked God to help her work through her negative feelings until she felt love. She stitched and stitched and prayed and prayed until she felt released from the anger. (She told me, "It ended up being a very big afghan!") She knew she needed to give a gift of sacrificial love, a piece of herself and her heart, or she'd never feel released from the bondage of her son's rejection. The afghan not only wrapped the new grandchild in love, it wrapped Jayne in God's protective care.

❀ ❀ ❀

Putting the Pieces Together

To be a woman God can use, one must be usable. What might be keeping you from being His envelope? Is it fear of failure? Criticism? Examine how you have handled failure in the past. Are there any changes that make you more able to hang in there or bounce back after a failure? How have you handled criticism in the past? Are there any changes you might want to make to keep you going as you deliver God's message of hope?

5

Everything in Its Place

*Why isn't there enough of
me to go around?*

Can you believe that average Americans, throughout our lifetimes, spend five years waiting in line, six months at red lights and one year playing telephone tag? We spend six years eating, one year searching for our belongings, eight months opening junk mail and four years doing housework![1] (Only four years?) In total, our personal care and travel (mostly back and forth to work) take up half of our lives![2]

Statistics show that women who are employed are working 233 more hours per year than women did in 1976. Women do two-thirds of the housework and four-fifths of the childcare.[3] Other surveys, however, dispute the claims of the whining, overworked masses, saying it isn't true they are working more hours. The average, in fact, is only working a 37-hour workweek.[4] While the average person's workweek may only be 37 hours, the same time analysts concur that certain groups work more: women in their 30s and 40s and those in the baby boom age range. However, today's 40-year-old still works less than a 40-year-old did in the same life stage 30 years ago.[5] Women tend to have four hours less free time than men each week.[6] Nearly 40 percent of people say they *feel* rushed.[7] In a study of time journals, where people wrote down how they actually spent their time, overall leisure time had been extended—however, it was usually in smaller increments—so nearly all of it went into watching TV.[8] Television may be the main reason many of us don't feel like we have more free time than before because we have nothing tangible to show for it.

"Some people are feeling overworked because they have more roles to play. . . In addition, work may seem longer now because its pace and anxiety level has intensified. The average worker today produces about 30 percent more goods and services than he or she did a generation ago. But the rewards don't seem to have kept pace with the pressures…Complaints about long workweeks are at least correct in the long, historical sense. Although today's workers may not be putting in the brutal 60-hour-plus workweeks common early in the Industrial Age, they're still working among the longest workweeks in human history. In the medieval era, for example, serfs worked long days in the fields but also had more than 100 holidays a year."[9]

Why are we so obsessed with saving time and using it effectively? Because time matters. A poem by an anonymous author was handed to me recently:

Every Moment

To realize the value of ONE YEAR,
Ask a student who has failed his exam.
To realize the value of ONE MONTH,
Ask a mother who has given birth to a premature baby.
To realize the value of ONE WEEK,
Ask the editor of a weekly paper.
To realize the value of ONE HOUR,
Ask lovers who are waiting to meet.
To realize the value of ONE MINUTE,
Ask someone who has missed a train or plane.
To realize the value of ONE SECOND,
Ask a person who has survived an accident.
To realize the value of ONE MILLISECOND,
Ask the person who has won a silver medal in the Olympics.

Time can be important.

Why Do We Feel So Pressured?

I think the Bible explains the reason why pretty clearly. James, Jesus' own brother, explains the dilemma by a statement of fact: "Why, you do not even know what will happen tomorrow. What is your life? You are a mist that appears for a little while and then vanishes" (James 4:14).

James is asking the same question we are. What is significant in life? "What is your life?" is a question that means "of what character is your life?" James then goes on to explain another of the "You are" statements in the Bible. *You are mist!*

We are all mist and we can't get out of it! A friend of mine who has had to deal with breast cancer several times has a wonderful answer when people express sadness over her diagnosis. She simply says, "It's okay, we are all terminal." Life is short, and the death rate is still 100 percent.

A poem was sent to my husband recently that captures the brevity of life:

> I read of a man who stood to speak
> at the funeral of his friend.
> He referred to the dates on her tombstone
> from the beginning...to the end.
>
> He noted that first came the date of her birth
> and spoke of the second with tears,
> but he said that what mattered most of all
> was the dash between those years.
>
> For that dash represents all the time
> that she spent alive on earth,
> and now only those who loved her know
> what that little line is worth.
>
> For it matters not, how much we own;
> the cars, the house, the cash.
> What matters is how we live and love
> and how we spend our dash.
>
> So think about this long and hard,
> are there things you'd like to change?
> For you never know how much time is left.
> (You could be at "dash mid-range.")
>
> If we could just slow down enough to consider
> what's true and what is real,
> and always try to understand
> the way other people feel.

And...be less quick to anger,
and show appreciation more
and love the people in our lives
like we've never loved before.

If we treat each other with respect,
and more often wear a smile,
remembering that this special dash
might only last a while.

So, when your eulogy is being read
with your life's actions to rehash...
would you be pleased with the things
they have to say about how you spent your dash?

Not only is life short, God has planned a lot in already! Life comes prepackaged by God. In Ecclesiastes 3:1-8, God says:

There is a time for everything,
and a season for every activity under heaven:
a time to be born and a time to die,
a time to plant and a time to uproot,
a time to kill and a time to heal,
a time to tear down and a time to build,
a time to weep and a time to laugh,
a time to mourn and a time to dance,
a time to scatter stones and a time to gather them,
a time to embrace and a time to refrain,
a time to search and a time to give up,
a time to keep and a time to throw away,
a time to tear and a time to mend,
a time to be silent and a time to speak,
a time to love and a time to hate,
a time for war and a time for peace.

A Clear Focus

As you can see, there isn't a lot of discretionary time in life. Since time is at a premium, how can we squeeze the most out of the little time we have in a way that will bring ultimate glory to God, provide for the needs of those we love and be personally fulfilling to ourselves?

Many of us feel so stretched, so frantic and so frenzied at the pace of life. How do we know when we are too busy? You know you're too busy when:

- Cleaning up the dining area means getting the fast-food bags out of the backseat of your car.

- Your reason for not staying in touch with family is that they do not have email addresses.

- You have a To Do list that includes entries for lunch and bathroom breaks and they are usually the ones that never get crossed off.

- You consider 2nd-day-air delivery painfully slow.

- You refer to your dining room table as the two-drawer lateral filing cabinet.

- Your idea of being organized is multiple colored Post-It® notes.

- Your grocery list has been on your refrigerator so long some of the products don't even exist any more.

- You get all excited when it's Saturday and you can wear sweats to work.

- You find you really need PowerPoint to explain what you do for a living.

- You think that "progressing an action plan" and "calendarizing a project" are acceptable topics for family meals.

- You know the people at the airport hotels better than your next door neighbors.

- You think a "half-day" means leaving at 5 o'clock.

- You think it's more strategic to buy clean underwear and socks than try to find any in your kids' rooms to wash.

You know you're feeling time is scarce, when you look around and see:

- Condensing of birthday parties into restaurant meals at which the wait staff assemble to sing a quick chorus of "Happy Birthday," perhaps accompanied by a cupcake with a candle extinguished within twenty seconds.

- Running of red lights, risking life and limb to save a few seconds.

- Using drive through windows...you drive through throwing money at them, they throw grease, salt and sugar back at you.

- Wrecking the car as a result of simultaneously driving, talking on the telephone, listening to a taped lecture and eating lunch out of a McDonald's bag.

- Following the new social taboos against being late, taking too long to get to the point in a conversation or waiting—for anything.[10]

We don't have to feel like we're trying to hold life together in the midst of a hurricane. There are a few things we can do to gain a sense of surety, confidence and the feeling of standing in a firm place.

God wants us to make the most of our time. He wants us to have a clear focus and a stable life in an unstable world. He even tells us we can do it. Twice, God says *You are standing firm.* Once as a warning: "So, if you think you are standing firm, be careful that you don't fall!" (1 Corinthians 10:12) and once as a compliment, a statement of fact: "For now we really live, since you are standing firm in the Lord" (1 Thessalonians 3:8).

Think about it. Our lives, even as frenzied and frantic as they are, can't be as bad as those living in the first century church. Because of the persecution of the church, at any moment families could be torn apart, businesses seized, believers could be jailed, beaten by an angry crowd, thrown into an arena to be eaten by lions or dashed to pieces by the horns of a wild bull. It was a war against Christians with no place to flee but to God. Yet still God proclaimed to those in Thessalonica, a church founded by Paul's teaching amidst controversy in the busy port city, "you are standing firm." How can we stand firm?

Paul sent Timothy to the Thessalonians to keep the people encouraged in their focus. To Corinth, Paul penned a letter full of warnings because they were a church losing their focus. In the letter to those in Thessalonica, we see Paul commending their focus:

> And we also thank God continually because, when you received the word of God, which you heard from us, you accepted it not as the word of men, but as it actually is, the word of God, which is at work in you who believe (1 Thessalonians 2:13).

> But Timothy has just now come to us from you and has brought good news about your faith and love. He has told us that you always have pleasant memories of us and that you long to see us, just as we also long to see you (1 Thessalonians 3:6).

Paul commends how they received the Word—then lived it out. In principle, it is simple but in practicality we have to battle life to stay focused. God tells us that we are children of promise

(Galatians 4:28). The context of this section of Scripture is the contrast between Ishmael and Isaac, two sons of Abraham. We are compared to being like Isaac, children of promise. A promise God gave Abraham (see Genesis 15:5) to give him a son and descendants as numerous as the stars. God also had a land for Abraham to possess. Key point: Abraham only received the blessing when he camped out on the promise. When Abraham fulfilled his purpose, he enjoyed the promise. When he forgot the promise, and took life into his own hands, then negative results followed. Conflict arose between his wife and the child of the promise and his maid and her child—a child conceived when the promise wasn't believed.

God has promises for us. He promises to give us a future and a hope (Jeremiah 29:11). He promises that truth will set us free (John 8:32). He promises that we will have an abundant life (John 10:10), a hope that will not disappoint (Romans 5:5) and joy and peace beyond comprehension (Philippians 4:7). Key point: When we fulfill God's purpose, we enjoy the blessing of those promises. So how can we sift through all of what life promises to live out the purpose God has for our lives?

There are a set of questions that I have used that helped me discover the purpose God has planned for me. Ask yourself these same questions:

What are you good at? List the top ten things you think you do well or enjoy doing. When you are wondering what your passion and calling is, remember God tends to use us most often in areas He has gifted us in. Deborah was a natural leader, so God made her a judge. Esther was beautiful, so God used her beauty to raise her to the platform of a queen who could save a nation. Priscilla loved to study and teach scripture, so when a young pastor came through town and his theology was a little incomplete, God used her to equip Apollos, who then went on to achieve a broader ministry himself. Every once in a while, God uses a seeming weakness: Moses confessed to being slow of speech. Well, maybe he felt that way because he'd been on the backside of a desert with sheep for 40 years, so he felt inadequate as a speaker, but before that he was trained in his day's best education in the palace of the Pharaoh. Who better to take God's message to the Pharaoh than one who'd been trained right alongside him?

Yes, Paul said, "But he said to me, 'My grace is sufficient for you, for my power is made perfect in weakness'...For when I am weak, then I am strong" (2 Corinthians 12:9-10). Paul did acknowledge his infirmities, his thorn in the flesh, but Paul was also keenly aware of his credentials. He lists them in Philippians 3:4-6:

> If anyone else thinks he has reasons to put confidence in the flesh, I have more: circumcised on the eighth day, of the people of Israel, of the tribe of Benjamin, a Hebrew of Hebrews; in regard to the law, a Pharisee; as for zeal, persecuting the church; as for legalistic righteousness, faultless.

God took Paul's résumé, changed Paul's attitude and built a ministry on the credentials Paul had already achieved. Paul was both a citizen and a follower of Christ. His Roman citizenship extended his ministry. His rank among the Jewish leaders gave him a hearing among a people that were writing off the early church. It's one thing to ignore a fisherman, it's another to ignore one of your own. Paul acknowledged what God had built into his life, then because he was humble, God used him.

After my book *Woman of Influence* came out, the first phone call I received was from a woman in a metropolitan city in the east who said, "Thank you, Pam! I've been a CPA for years and I never could see how God might use me as an accountant! But since I've read your book, I have felt compelled to start a battered women's shelter in our community and I see how my accounting and business background will really help!"

Did God make her good with money for a reason? Definitely! And will God use the gifts she is good at? Yes! Before a ministry to battered women can even begin, they need a building, funds and ongoing supporters. Will people be more likely to give their hard-earned money to someone who is certified to take good care of money? Absolutely! God knows the talents, gifts and strengths you have and He wants to maximize them for His purposes and plans.

When I had to make a choice on how I would use my college degree, I saw a variety of options: elementary, secondary or high school teacher; college professor; freelance writer; journalist for a paper or magazine; speaker; director of women at a church or dean of women; editor; at-home mom; public relations or advertising. Writing, speaking and leading came to the surface when I asked myself, *What three things do I think I do best?* My question then became, "What would make best use of these three?"

Look at the pie chart (Multiplicity Figure 1) on page 111. By spending your time developing the skills that are most portable, it can save you time because you are more focused. For example, those students who have a clear direction in college complete their course work in a shorter amount of time than those who keep changing their major. Those same focused students also know what internships and practical experiences they need to create a résumé and receive the training they need for entrance into the job market. It takes valuable time to travel up and down rabbit trails in life. Focus will save you time. In my diagram, the core skills of writing and speaking would be the best portable skills to hone no matter what career change I might have to make.

In an environment of corporate downsizing, constantly shifting markets and unstable economy, modern women need an abundance of portable skills in order to accomplish their linear

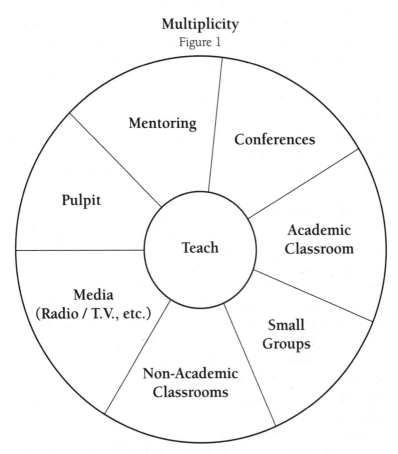

Multiplicity
Figure 1

Use your same talent or gift in a variety of settings

goals. The key word in today's world is change! Flexibility and adaptability are key components of goals today and in the future. With persistence, dreams can be achieved by gathering portable skills that will help you anticipate and navigate change.

If this is a hard question, ask your friends and family: What am I good at? What do I seem to enjoy? What do I talk about the most? Where your mouth is, your heart tends to be too!

God says: Now you are the body of Christ, and each one of you is a part of it (1 Corinthians 12:27). The context of this verse is that God gives gifts to each member of the body of Christ. You are just as necessary as every other person in the body of Christ because *you are gifted!*

What are you not good at? What don't you enjoy? It is just as important to know what *not* to do as what *to do!* List on a yellow pad a few things in life that you'd rather not do.

I'm not great in the kitchen—no, Julia Child I am not. I do like to have people in my home, but I have found through experience that I would rather have someone stay for a short while (like a week max!) rather than long term (months or years). Because our world has so many people in it, I find that Bill and I need our home to be a place where there are fewer people expectations.

Does this mean that I never cook, that I never have people stay over? No, it just means that as much as possible I try to do what God has equipped me to do. I may not bake cookies for my children's classroom parties—but because I want to be an involved mother, I will write press releases for their school or teach a writing workshop. What are the two or three things that stress you out the most?

Saying no isn't always easy. What are some ways to graciously bow out when you feel you aren't called—but you are being recruited?

10 ways to graciously say no to people:

1. That sounds like a wonderful opportunity, I wish I had time. I'm sure someone else will receive the blessing of being involved.

2. Oh, normally I'd love to, but my plate is full. Can you check back with me next time?

3. Wow, that sounds like just the thing _____ might enjoy.

4. I won't be able to, but if you call me in a few days I might have some people I could recommend who would be willing and interested.

5. Let me check my calendar. If you call me in 24 hours I'll give you a definite answer.

6. You must be so good at what you do! You deserve some people who will be of your same caliber, and I'm afraid I'm not one of them in this area. I would, however, be willing to _____ (make an offer that would fit with your life).

7. Oh, I'm so disappointed! Please place me on the list to contact next time (next year, etc.)

8. No, I can't do that this time. I know I've disappointed you. I know this may even put you in a bind. I'm just going to ask you to give me grace this time. There may be a time I can do the same for you.

9. Please forgive me because I'm going to have to say no.

10. You are such a wonderful person. You know I love you like a (sister, son, daughter, etc.) but I am going to have to say no this time.

What is your time worth? Is working outside the home really helping you financially? Write out how much it costs you to work. Include items such as child care costs, wardrobe, lunches out, extra car or extra wear and tear, and convenience food or eating out. You may find that you aren't earning as much as you thought. When our three boys were preschoolers, Bill and I did an exercise that indicated the income I would have to earn was larger than his take-home pay—plus I would have missed out on so many intangible and precious moments that the price simply wasn't worth it. Try looking at your talents through different paradigms, like working from home, tag-team parenting, part-time employment, and so on. Saying no to a method of working might help you say yes to other priorities.

On the other hand, it might be more advantageous to hire out some tasks to buy more time for the people and activities you love most. Let's say you decide it takes you 15 hours a week to keep your house up the way you want it. If you worked a few extra hours at work, or made one more sale, or budgeted differently, you might be able to hire household help and cut your hours of housekeeping down to three to four per week—gaining a much-needed day off. I find the biggest hurdle some women face is the social or personal pressure they feel thinking they have to do all the housework. Try journaling your spending habits for a month. You might decide to say no to some expenses in order to say yes to some priorities.

Sometimes, it's just a temporary no. I try to look at my life through the prism of the seasons. I end one responsibility, like chairing the winter retreat, before I take on the role of team mom in the spring. This means I am not a team mom during basketball, but I might be during baseball. Sometimes these are temporary yeses too. Because I drive my son to Student Venture each Tuesday, I maximize my time by volunteering to drive his friends, and thus I gain an inside scoop on his life. Since I am there anyway, I often volunteer for smaller servant-type assignments during that hour.

What are my successes? Write five to seven paragraphs and describe times you served others (work, volunteer work, ministry) and you felt it went well (people were helped, encouraged, changed). Why did you enjoy it? Why do you think it went well? (Feel free to go as far back in time as you'd like to.) After you write all the paragraphs, then circle or underline any common words or themes.

When I did this activity, I realized that I love to serve best when I am free to be a visionary leader. I love creating something out of nothing. Once things start running smoothly or if things get to be a routine or in a rut—I am bored and want a new challenge. So the best use of my leadership and speaking gifts are when I am allowed to have free rein. That's why it suits me to be in charge of an organization—especially one I created to accomplish a pre-determined goal. I am more fulfilled in a plan that is flexible enough to allow me new challenges. The church where I serve is a good fit because they are very open to giving me the freedom to run with ideas.

Another pattern I saw when I wrote my paragraphs was the word "teach." It was used over and over, but never in a "routine" teaching setting where the schedule is the same day in and day out, or I teach the same material for 25 years! I love to teach when I can also be innovative.

What is my uniqueness? There are some things you do that most people don't do as well as you or with the style and flair you have! Your uniqueness sets you apart. It may be the apple pie you make (and the love that goes into it). It could be your art, your speech, your hospitality, your clear thinking.

Author Daisy Hepburn recommends that you "Do first that which only you can do."[11] I am the only one who can love my husband. (Or else we'll make the tabloid headlines too.) I am the only one that can love my children. Other people can clean my house if necessary—but they can't nurture and train those young hearts. What things do you do that no one else can do?

Leadership expert John Maxwell encourages delegation. If someone else does what you do 80 percent as well, Maxwell encourages delegation at this point. We are then free to do that 20 percent that is unique to us. For example, other moms can work lunch-yard duty—but few moms can work with businesses to secure grants and donations. I try to spend the majority of my time doing what is unique to me.

When Bill and I were building our home, the project lasted a lot longer than we thought, so our finances were stretched to the limit. For a time, I thought we might lose the house we'd worked so hard to build. I remember praying in a quiet time, "God, I'm so frustrated. I can't believe this is happening. We've worked so long and hard, especially Bill. I could get really angry at him. He led us into this. But God, he's the best thing going in my life apart from You. I have had more opportunities to talk about You, Lord, because of the love Bill and I share than anything else. So God, I'm going to choose, right now. I could nag Bill, whine, complain, panic or do a lot of other things—but I won't, even though I feel like it. So God, even if I lose this house, or if we lose our church because we lost the house, then I'll take that, but I will not let these current setbacks separate me from Bill. I won't let them separate me from You."

At that moment, I *knew* what I had with Bill wasn't just good, it was unique. We had a love that would last. Within a year, we were given our first opportunity to write about relationships—and we still live in the house that Bill built.

One way to make the most of the uniqueness that God has built into your life is the practice of multipliicty (Look at Figure 2, page 117). By taking your strongest uniqueness and using it in as many ways as possible, you save valuable time and you are a better steward of the time and talent God gave you. For example, if I write a magazine article on marital communication, it can also be part of a chapter of a book, or trimmed to fit in a newspaper, or it could be part of our radio show or a section of a conference. It could also go on a web site or in a video series. One writing assignment has now been used seven different ways and hundreds of more people can be encouraged by the same message sent out in many directions. How can you use your talent in another setting

Multiplicity
Figure 2

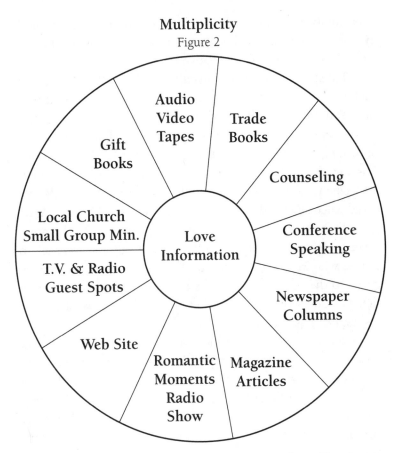

Use the same information in a variety of applications

or in a slightly different way to encourage more people or save more of your valuable time?

My friend Jesse Dillenger is a marriage and family counselor, and she encourages her clients to ask, "What will bring God maximum glory?" You might need to delegate so that your unique talents are best used, use multiplicity to expand your time or talents, or simplify part of your life. This way you will have more time in the area you are most effective in touching lives and providing an opportunity for change and growth for God. If we want to be used by God, we can't be afraid of opportunity just because the people around us may be afraid of change.

What spiritual markers do you remember? Often by looking back we can see how God has uniquely prepared us for our passion. You might have been raised with more than one language, in another culture or have special training. God is also the master of turning a pain into a platform for ministry. The burning bush was a marker to Moses. He knew that God had talked to him at a specific period of time. Moses had other markers too. He was saved when all the other baby boys were killed by Pharaoh. As he grew, he had to have asked the question, "Why me? Why was I saved?" He was educated in Egypt. When God sent him back to Egypt, who in all of Israel would have been better prepared to speak to the ruler than someone raised in the palace? Even the detail of God sparing his life when he struck down the Egyptian taskmaster was a marker.

God places clues in every life and as we look for them, we gain wisdom on how to focus our lives. You can't do everything—you are only one person. God built the markers into your life for a reason. He uses them to direct your path. Winston Churchill recounted, "I felt as if I were walking with destiny, and that all my past life had been but a preparation for this hour and for this trial."[12]

I have a few markers in my life. My mother put me in a speech contest when I was nine years old. I did a speech on "The Parts of a Lamb" and it won a gold medal. Because they recognized I had potential, my mom and grandmother took me to all the volunteer and philanthropic groups they were a part of and I either did a speech, a song, dance or gymnastics routine. I became comfortable in front of a crowd. While most people would rather do anything other than speak in front of a group, I am at home there. Then when I reflect on the number of teaching experiences I have had, I know that I was meant to impart information. All those experiences in my past are markers to lead me into a focus for my future. Graham Greene writes, "There is always one moment in childhood when the door opens and lets the future in."[13]

Markers can also direct you to the people group(s) God wants you to reach. Bill and I met in college at a student leadership conference. Most couples don't marry at 20. And most never get the great training in relational skills Bill and I received. Most aren't given the opportunity to teach and train others in those skills beginning the first day they get home from their honeymoon! Opportunities are a marker.

Luke 12:48 explains the importance of being a steward of the markers in your life: "From everyone who has been given much, much will be demanded; and from the one who has been entrusted with much, much more will be asked."

What legacy do I want to leave? When my grandmother died, all of her grandchildren drove or flew in from all over the country. We hadn't communicated about what each of us would say. We did not know what the other was going to say at the funeral. As each one of us came to the podium with what we had prepared, it became obvious what my grandmother's legacy was. All of us, using a variety of words, said the same things about my grandmother—she was so hospitable. She always took the time to offer homemade cookies and either milk or coffee to anyone who stopped by. People knew they would always have a place to stay the night—or two—or more if they needed a roof over their heads. She was a great cook, and a terrific cheerleader for her grandchildren's dreams. Even though she never completed her own high school education, she encouraged her grandchildren to complete their college degrees and lived to see five diplomas hanging on the wall.

What do you want said about you at your funeral? Each day you are living the legacy you are wanting to leave.

What is your mission? If you use the above questions, the answers should help lead you to your mission, your focus in life. Try to summarize what you learned from the above questions into a mission statement that explains what you will do, what you want to do, what you commit to do. Here is an example of the mission statement Bill and I decided upon early in our marriage.

> We, Bill and Pam Farrel, have a desire to fulfill the Great Commission through using our skills in professional ministry, with a focus of using the communication gifts God has given us. We are committed to personal discipleship as a lifestyle. We want our home to be an oasis where those who enter can see Christ at work in our marriage and family and where they can find hope. We, the Farrels, are committed to fun and friendships. We value people more than things. We prefer memories over material goods. We are committed to raise our children in such a way as they have the opportunity to know the benefits of personally knowing Jesus and walking with Him. We are committed to helping them discover their talents and equipping them to help fulfill the Great Commission and to have fun and a fulfilling life while doing so.

This mission statement serves as a grid. When opportunities cross my desk, I run them through the grid to see if they are worthy of a high place on my priority list. Because of our mission statement, opportunities that allow us to impact others to come to know God personally are highest on the list. Near the top is also memory-making for our marriage and family, friendship building, and using our communication gifts.

It isn't always easy to live with the decisions that a mission statement makes clear—but its use is strategic. When the opportunity to write our first book presented itself, we had yet to put a yard in. Our fence was nearly complete but not quite. But because people are more important than things, and because communicating in a way that builds marriages and families is a priority, we took a break from finishing the fence and yard. My fence may not ever impact someone's life for God, but I know the book already has.

Making these choices is not simple but it is imperative. Dr. Archibald Hart says, "We have to be firm with those who would clutter up our lives with trivia. We must be clear about our own priorities so we can make good decisions about what we will and will not do."[14]

The urgent can become a tyrannical taskmaster. Dr. Hart and a colleague were working on a project with a deadline. It seemed important to them both that the job be done well—but efficiently. Dr. Hart reminded his partner one day, "We need to get it done quickly!" That night Dr. Hart stood over the lifeless body of his friend. His colleague had had a heart attack that afternoon. "Suddenly, my 'We need to get it done quickly!' no longer had meaning. Death has a way of reordering priorities...we move from a worm's eye view to a bird's eye view."[15] A sense of personal mission will squeeze more out of life—and it will help tune your ear to the voice of God. By weighing out the answers to the above questions before God, you are given a framework from Christ. Every decision is then run through the framework, again saving time, and energy—energy that might have been spent on worrying before! Focus helps you invest in the life God gave you. Focus helps you spend your time wisely. Lillian Dickenson said, "Life is a coin. You can spend it anyway you wish, but you can spend it only once."

When I pace myself and base decisions on my mission, I gain the ability to "step back" and get a big picture. I can then make choices to find my place in God's plan. When I take the time to see what God has already done in my life, the pieces of life fall into place more easily. When I look at the pieces God has already laid down in my life, life doesn't look like such a puzzle anymore.

Putting the Pieces Together

Write a mission statement by using the answers to all the above questions. Post the statement somewhere you can see it often so you can naturally reinforce your decision-making grid.

6

A Precious Place

Does anyone appreciate me?

One day a man came home from work to find total mayhem at home. The kids were outside, still in their pajamas, playing in the mud and muck. There were empty food boxes and wrappers all around. As he proceeded into the house, he found an even bigger mess inside—dishes on the counter, dog food spilled on the floor, a broken glass under the table and a small pile of sand by the back door. The family room was strewn with toys and various items of clothing, and a lamp had been knocked over.

He hurried up the stairs, stepping over more toys, looking for his wife. He was becoming worried that she might be ill or that something had happened to her. He found her in the bedroom, still in bed with her pajamas on, reading a book. She looked up at him, smiled, and asked how his day went. He looked at her bewildered and asked "What happened here today?"

She smiled at him again and answered, "You know everyday when you come home from work and ask me what I did today?"

"Yes," he said.

She grinned. "Well, today I didn't do it!"

This is something most women feel at sometime or another. The laundry doesn't thank us for scrubbing their backs. The dishes don't praise us for the Jacuzzi we fix for them on a daily basis. The towels and sheets don't salute when we walk by.

I did an estimate to see what the financial worth of a homemaker would be if a family had to pay for the typical services mom renders year after year:

Housekeeping	$13,000	(20 hours a week for 52 weeks)
Nursing	$1,300	(1 hour a week for 52 weeks)
Cook	$21,840	(3 hours a day, 7 days a week, for 52 weeks)
Psychologist	$36,400	(1 hour a day, 7 days a week, for 52 weeks)
Taxi	$21,840	(3 hours a day, 7 days a week, for 52 weeks)
Tutor	$3,900	(1 hour a day, 5 days a week, for 52 weeks)
Party Planner	$22,500	(10 times a year spending 10 hours each party)
Sec./Receptionist	$17,472	(3 hours a day, 7 days a week, for 52 weeks)
Total	$138,252	

As you can see, most of us can't even afford ourselves! (And I didn't include the romantic things we do for our husbands if we are married. I didn't even want to go there!) And if you add all the hours up, it comes out to about a 35-hour day! We just *feel* like we have 35-hour days when we serve our family because it is so easy for them—and for us—to forget how valuable we are to them.

Okay, some of us get the perks of peanut-butter kisses from tousled-haired children, or the occasional thank you grunt of an adolescent who briefly frees herself from the bathroom mirror. There are some of you who get a card, or maybe even a gift from that wonderful husband who has noticed that only you have radar for whatever he happens to have lost in the house! However, for many of us, it is easy to slide into the "Does anyone appreciate me?" mode after a hard day.

Carla, a busy working mother, shares, "In a two-career family, the time to prepare dinner is limited. One evening I was opening cans of soup and mushrooms and pouring the mixture into a ready-made pie-crust shell. My teen-age son walked in and asked, 'What's for dinner?'

"'Homemade pot pie,' I responded. 'Well, maybe,' he said, watching me juggling the cans. 'But "home assembled" might be more like it.'"[1] Some of you may also not feel valued at the job that takes you outside of your home. Dilbert cartoons have become bestsellers, in part because they capture the frustration of the daily disrespect many of us experience on the job. In one cartoon, a manager says, "I think you could all take a lesson in corporate respect from What's-his-face here."[2] There are many days we each feel like ol' what's-her-face!

Because we all long for R-E-S-P-E-C-T, we can fall into the false trap of looking in the wrong place for our affirmation. We cannot depend on our husband, our children, friends, parents or boss to give us the validation, affirmation and reassurance we are looking for. Even if we are surrounded by positive and affirming people, their words will help some, but still not fill the void in our hearts. That void can only be filled by hearing from God and believing in His view of us.

You Are More Valuable than Birds

Growing up on a farm in Idaho, there were times that our entire phone and electrical lines were wing to wing with miles and miles of magpies! The sound of those cackling, screeching birds was deafening. At times, a flock chatting to each other would drown out the sound of our television set! Dad would then go outside and shoot a BB gun in the air to send them flying to someone else's backyard.

There are times when we might feel a little like those birds. We chat on about our day, only to have our husband say, "So what's the bottom line here?" or "Get to the point." Or we try to share our thoughts with our children, only to be shut out or worse, "Did you say something, Mom?" We step out in a group to share an idea or opinion and it is received with a roll of eyes or a "Next!" Some days we feel like we are being "shooed away" and sent packing. We wonder if anyone values our input or if we really do sound as worthless as a cackling bird.

God cares. He made sure we would know how much He valued us when Jesus declared in the Sermon on the Mount, "Consider the ravens: They do not sow or reap, they have no storeroom or barn; yet God feeds them. And how much more valuable you are than birds!" (Luke 12:24).

Did he say ravens? Are you sure it wasn't the peacocks only that He cares for? Or the chickens—at least they produce a marketable product. No, it was ravens. Ravens are part of the crow family. They are scavengers, feeding off the dead, and they fly like a buzzard. In other words, ravens are the bottom feeders of the sky. And God still cares for their needs.

But Jesus didn't stop there. He wanted to make sure we got the point. So He looks around him again, and spots an everyday flower. He says, "Consider how the lilies grow. They do not labor or spin. Yet I tell you, not even Solomon in all his splendor was dressed like one of these" (Luke 12:27).

Now these weren't the lilies that we use for special events like weddings and Easter. No, they weren't the gorgeous huge single blossoming flowers of triumph. These were field lilies—much closer in value to our dandelions. They were everywhere. Yet Jesus parallels them to Solomon dressed in all of his kingly splendor.

So how did Solomon dress? No ancient ruler, with perhaps the exception of Alexander the Great, had as much at his fingertips as Solomon. His kingdom was expansive, and monarchs from the entire eastern world traded with him. The Queen of Sheba visited him and a Pharaoh's daughter was a wife. Solomon had the best fabrics, the newest and most novel bangles, bracelets and beads available. He had more gold, silver and jewels than any previous ruler. Those working in his court, including those in charge of his attire, would have been the best available at the time and may have traveled a great distance just to serve this majestic king. It would be like having the entire fashion industry at your beck and call.

What Jesus is saying is that we—normal, everyday, regular us—are as beautiful and valuable to Him as a king in full regalia. We look better to God than a supermodel on a runway in Paris or New York. We are better than a designer label to our Designer.

Yep, you got it. Even in that Kmart blue-light-special flowered housecoat, He says you are valuable. Even on the day you sneak to the grocery store in your painting clothes and baseball cap, He thinks you are special. On bad hair days, good hair days—or no hair days—he thinks you are special.

But because the average person has to hear something at least three times to remember it, God says one more time: "If that is how God clothes the grass of the field, which is here today, and tomorrow is thrown into the fire, how much more will he clothe you, O you of little faith!" (Luke 12:28).

He reminds us that yes, we are finite. Our death will come as sure as the grass in the field. But God cared enough about grass— *grass*—to clothe it in that beautiful green. He made that wonderful stuff that we love to walk barefoot on. The green carpet we get to mow—and secretly love the smell of its clippings. He says, even though we are finite, and even expendable, (there are other blades of grass) He still cares enough to color our world, clothe us and use us to make the world a better place.

So to sum it all up, from this passage we can surmise that because God cares about the bottom-of-the-barrel birds, the common-as-they-come flowers and the there's-plenty-more-of-it grass, and He does it in a personal way, God will care for us. He will care for us even when we feel so low we could walk under a door, or so common we wouldn't even be noticed at a family reunion or as dispensable as a paper cup. No matter how we feel about ourselves, God says we're valuable and He will care for our needs personally.

Most of us can handle it if our face doesn't grace the cover of a magazine or our name doesn't make it up in lights. But sometimes, when we don't get the raise we've been banking on, when there is a pile of wet towels and dirty clothes on the bathroom floor, when we come home night after night to an empty apartment, we can start to wonder if anyone even knows we exist.

Some of us are in careers that make us realize that we struggle with envy, jealousy or the "why not me?" syndrome. A professor friend of mine owns a T-shirt that says *Publish or Perish*. Some of us feel invisible to those in charge. The more media driven our world becomes, the more likely it is that we will feel sidelined, unimportant or insignificant. If we don't have a web page, an email address or a cell phone number we might not feel in touch, but it only gets worse when we can begin to believe the lie that no one wants to be in touch with us. Some days we may feel like the sum total of our life boils down to a nine-digit ID number.

Amy Roth, a new friend of mine in ministry, lives and ministers under the shadow of Nashville's Music Row. In a city filled with big names and exceptional musicians all waiting for a big break, it is easy to begin to wonder if anyone even knows your talent, your hopes, your dreams or the song you have in your heart. Amy and some friends penned a song that captured my heart the first time I heard it at a conference where I spoke. God knows my name and yours.

He Knows My Name

Like a drop of rain in the ocean, that the tide has set in motion
He knows my name, He knows my name
Like a single blade of grass, hidden in a meadow vast
He knows my name, He knows my name

Like a star in the Milky Way, never noticed in the light of day
He knows my name, He knows my name
Like a single grain of sand, blowing in a barren land
He knows my name, He knows my name

Treasure may elude me
I may never get a taste of fame
Yet if I don't go down in history
I don't have to be ashamed
'Cause He knows my name, He knows my name

Though there are times
When I feel sad and small
Feeling no worth at all
Jesus understands

Through knowing eyes
He sees me differently
Giving me the faith to place my life within His hands

Someday I will stand before Him, with the thousands I'll adore Him
He knows my name, He knows my name
When the book of life is opened, before a word is ever spoken
He knows my name, He knows my name
He knows my name, He knows my name

Treasure may elude me
I may never get a taste of fame
Yet if I don't go down in history
I don't have to be ashamed
'Cause He knows my name, He knows my name
He knows my name, He knows my name[3]

So what's the catch? How can we see ourselves this same wonderful way God does?

Don't Worry!

After Jesus describes how valuable we are, He gives us the secret to remembering it! "And do not set your heart on what you will eat or drink; do not worry about it. For the pagan world runs after all such things, and your Father knows that you need them. But seek his kingdom, and these things will be given to you as well" (Luke 12:29-31).

Try this: Each time you are tempted to worry, refocus on what God says about you. For example, when Bill and I had resigned from our youth ministry position, but had yet to be chosen for a senior pastorate, Bill freelanced as a draftsman. Well if you've ever owned your own business you know it can easily be feast or famine—or as in our case, Bill was consistently busy with work, but clients weren't paying him in a timely manner. I had a list on our refrigerator of our needs—not *wants* but *needs*: food items, diaper and clothing needs for the boys, bills that needed paying, things like that. Each day I would look at that list and force down a rising sense of panic. The only thing that helped was to tell myself, *God sees, God knows. I'll seek Him. We'll work our hardest at what He's called us to today and He'll take care of the rest because I'm more valuable than the birds, more valuable than the flowers, more valuable than the grass. There's still birds, flowers and grass—and that means that God is still watching over them.* Then I'd tell myself, *Pam, don't worry about when God will take care of these things. You focus on obeying Him and not worrying about these things for the next hour.* I knew I couldn't even think about going another day without some of those things—so I just concentrated on being content without them for the next hour. I could survive an hour—so hour after hour, day after day, that's what I did. In God's timing the list was taken care of and many other lists, often with bigger things on them, have come and gone. But by seeing myself as valuable in God's sight, I gained the ability to be positive even in a negative situation.

Sometimes I wondered if it was faith or just denial. But I have decided it was faith, because denial would be to pretend the list didn't exist, or act as if we had all the money in the world, but I did neither. I just focused on the Creator of the world and His opinion of me. I then gained the ability to trust that He would create a way for me to endure the circumstance and provide a way out of the situation in His time—and He did.

You Are Heirs

While I wrote this book, I was also serving as the executrix for my father's estate. I have become all too aware of what it means to be an heir. The part most people look forward to is the inheritance—the money—but what most people don't realize is that with the money comes responsibility.

Part of my job as the executrix was to ensure that all my father's accounts, debts and taxes were discharged with integrity. It was my job to preserve his good name with his creditors. I also oversaw the disbursement of inheritance monies to each person named in the Will. I know with the money that was given to me came an emotional weight of how to spend or save it wisely. This was a one-time gift. My dad wasn't going to come back to earth and live another life and leave me money again. This was a one-time shot and my family trusted me to be wise.

That seems to be a little of what God is saying when He calls us heirs. "And you are heirs of the prophets and of the covenant God made with your fathers. He said to Abraham, 'Through your offspring all peoples on earth will be blessed'" (Acts 3:25).

Yes, we have an amazing inheritance—but it comes with a P.S.: *By the way, you have one life—use it wisely.* Henrietta Mears, the founder of Forest Home conference center and a leader who discipled many future leaders, said, "What you are is God's gift to you. What you become is your gift to God."

What does God give to us? What is the inheritance?

> I pray also that the eyes of your heart may be enlightened in order that you may know the hope to which he has called you, the riches of his glorious inheritance in the saints, and his incomparably great power for us who believe. That power is like the working of his mighty strength, which he exerted in Christ when he raised him from the dead and seated him at his right hand in the heavenly realms, far above all rule and authority, power and dominion, and every title that can be given, not only in the present age but also in the one to come (Ephesians 1:18-21).

Wow! Did you catch that? "His incomparably great power is available to us who believe"—the same power that raised Christ from the dead. Christ, who sits "far above all rule and authority, power or dominion," is available to help us with our life. Christ, who is given "every title that can be given, not only in the present age but also in the one to come," can help you and me when we struggle with our worth. That's why it is the "hope" to which we're called. That's why it is a "glorious inheritance." It's glorious because God's power, ability, creativity and strength are there to help us walk the walk we are called to. God doesn't point to His place for us and say, "Good luck, hope you can pull it off!" No, God leads us to be usable by living the calling through us by His spirit, and that pulls the pieces together. My life falls into place with more clarity, and less frustration, when I am relying on His power rather than my own.

Your Fair Share

God wants to make sure we know that the inheritance was fair. He tells us the spiritual playing field has been made even. "There is neither Jew nor Greek, slave nor free, male nor female, for you are all one in Christ Jesus. If you belong to Christ, then you are Abraham's seed, and heirs according to the promise" (Galatians 3:28-29).

We are all *Abraham's seed. You are one in Christ.* The point is that "in Christ" distinctions do not exist. Christ is so pervasive in His impact on our identity that all the other indications of who we are pale into insignificance. Race, national distinctions, class differences, political alliances and sexual genetics are small considerations compared to the hope and transformation that exists in Christ. Our nationality, gender and initial economic position are chosen for us and create division. "Belonging to Christ" is a choice each of us makes and results in adoption and glory.

You are Abraham's seed is a reference to the promise made to Abraham regarding Isaac. Isaac was a gift from God based on His promise rather than Abraham's performance. When we give our hearts to Christ we get in line with the promise of God that is dependent on His faithfulness rather than on our performance.

We have all we need in Him. Looking for success? You already have it. No inheritance can match the one you already have. Looking for identity? Look again at the "You Are" list that comes after Chapter 1. That list describes you and me! We just have to walk in it. Looking for emotional connection? Your Creator wants a friendship, a relationship with you. Looking for security? Nothing can take any of this away from us! "Though the fig tree does not bud, and there are no grapes on the vines, though the olive crop fails and the fields produce no food, though there are no sheep in the pen and no cattle in the stalls, yet I will rejoice in the Lord, I will be joyful in God my Savior. The Sovereign Lord is my strength; he makes my feet like the feet of a deer, he enables me to go on the heights" (Habakkuk 3:17-19).

No matter what happens, the Lord will be our strength. God will love us through anything. "No, in all these things we are more than conquerors through him who loved us. For I am convinced that neither death nor life, neither angels nor demons, neither the present nor the future, nor any powers, neither height nor depth, nor anything else in all creation, will be able to separate us from the love of God that is in Christ Jesus our Lord" (Romans 8:37-39).

A New Question

Maybe we are asking the wrong question. Instead of asking if anyone appreciates me, I will get further in life and be more usable to God if I ask, "Am I pursuing the opportunities I have in front of me?"

Mary McLeod Bethune was born the fifteenth of seventeen children. Her parents were freed slaves living in the south and she was born two years before reconstruction ended. Her family had to be reassembled from various plantations in South Carolina. Mary worked the cotton fields as a child on what her family called "the homestead." She attended Marysville Presbyterian Mission School, and was a prized pupil of that one-room school. She won a scholarship to Scotia Seminary and upon graduation she was awarded a scholarship to Moody's Institute for Home and Foreign Missions in Chicago where she was the only black student. She dreamt of returning to Africa to minister to the spiritual and intellectual needs of the people there; however, she was informed that there were no openings for black missionaries in Africa.

Mary could have felt like a person without a country. She was a black woman who wasn't allowed to serve in Africa, yet she was not even considered a citizen yet by the country in which she was born. Mary lived somewhere in between.

Just like Mary, at times we all have felt like we're in limbo, not comfortable in this world but still here instead of heaven. However, citizenship of heaven, the greatest privilege and the most challenging calling, is its own promised land. Paul understood this when he wrote: "Consequently, you are no longer foreigners and aliens, but fellow citizens with God's people and members of God's household" (Ephesians 2:19).

You are fellow citizens. You have all the rights God gives you. Here's the catch—there is only one right listed in the New Testament: "But as many as received him, to them he gave the *right* to become children of God, even to those who believe in his name" (John 1:12 NASB, emphasis added). You are members of *God's household.* (God also says you are sons and sons of God.[4]) We're God's kids. "Now you, brothers, like Isaac, are children of promise" (Galatians 4:28). *You are children of promise*, a promise come true!

God promised Isaac to Sarah. He promised Abraham that He would bless the nations through his son. Against all odds, God made the promise—and kept it. In the face of difficulty, God makes promises to us and keeps them. We don't have to be worried that someone will step on our rights—they will. But they can't take away the promises of God because God has control over them.

Stepping into the Promise

Mary Bethune was not one to stay discouraged. She returned to Marysville to become an assistant teacher of her home school, then she received an appointment to the Haines Institute in Augusta, Georgia. It was at Haines that Mary experienced a primarily female educational setting. Her mentor there, Lucey Laney, ran an excellent girl's school and helped found a hospital. Mary's one year of experience at Haines would serve her well in the future.

She married, had a son, and continued her mission work by starting a school in Palatka, Florida where she stayed for five years. Then, at the encouragement of a pastor, she started Daytona Literary and Industrial School for girls. For the next twenty years, Mary divided her time between making the school a success and stepping into public leadership on a national level.

She led a drive to register black voters (which earned her a visit from the Ku Klux Klan). She was elected president of the State Federation of Colored Women's Clubs where she organized a movement to combat school segregation. She became the eighth president of the prestigious National Association of Colored Women's Clubs and it was under her leadership a national headquarters was acquired in Washington, D.C. She was called by President Calvin Coolidge to attend a Child Welfare Conference. Under Herbert Hoover's presidential administration she attended the National Commission for Child Welfare, the Hoover Commission on Home Building and Home Ownership and was appointed to the planning committee established by the Federal

Office of Education of Negroes. Finally, she was appointed to be an advisor on minority affairs in the Roosevelt administration.

Eleanor Roosevelt invited her to a luncheon for representative leaders of the National Council of Women of the United States. It was at this luncheon that her lifelong friendship with the mother of the president began. During this same time her school enlarged to become a high school, then a junior college and finally it merged with a boys college to become Bethune-Cookman College. She was a bright businesswoman and civic activist who worked tirelessly to improve the world in which she was born. In her weekly column in the *Chicago Defender* newspaper, Mary wrote her opinion of the *Plessy v. Fergeson* Supreme Court Decision which unraveled the separate but equal doctrine that had been in place most of her life. She wrote:

> There can be no divided democracy, no class government, no half-free country, under the Constitution. Therefore, there can be no discrimination, no segregation, no separation of some citizens from the rights which belong to all...We are on our way. But these are frontiers which we must conquer.[5]

Her heart is seen in one of her many quotes, "Invest in the human soul. Who knows, it might be a diamond in the rough."[6]

Trailblazers usually aren't appreciated when they are forging a new path. It may be years before the contribution you are making for people is noticed or appreciated. It may not even be appreciated this side of heaven, but it is still important.

Creating an Opportunity

Mary Bethune looked at the need and created an opportunity. Murie Strode said, "Do not follow where the path may lead. Go instead where there is no path and leave a trail." Mary didn't wait to be appreciated. She stepped out and did what God appreciates—she invested in people.

Eugenia Sanderson has done the same thing. When she retired from her job as Director of Dietetics of Sharp Hospital, Eugenia gave up her car and with it a host of activities that had kept her busy. Instead of sitting on the sidelines and letting depression settle in, eighty-five-year-old Eugenia came up with a plan. "I decided to quit thinking about what I couldn't do and start thinking about what I can do—and I can ice cookies, so I started doing that."

Each day Eugenia ices and decorates cookies, then heads out to her driveway just when the elementary school up the street is letting out. "I noticed they came by. All I had to do was stand out there with a pan of cookies and they came." Word spread quickly. For ten years, every school day, every child that passes gets to sample one of "Grandma Jean's treats."

Grandma Jean makes sure each child receives a parent letter of introduction and a card with her name and phone number on it so parents can "check her out." Each Friday, Eugenia invites the youngsters into her open garage for a Bible story and refreshments.

Eugenia's neighbor Diane Reichs says the neighborhood is delighted with Grandma Jean. "She's just real loving. She's like everyone's grandma."

Eugenia's relatives now give her cookies for Christmas and birthdays so she can give them away. Eugenia never married, never had children of her own. "I've traveled a lot and I have a lot of pretty things I've collected. And I could part with them. But I can't part with my kids...I know there's a good many days when I wouldn't even dress if I didn't have to go out there to hand out cookies."[7]

What these two women, who were separated by centuries, found was that you may not always be appreciated, but you can be effective. Of course we would all like to be appreciated and effective at the same time. If you have to choose between the two, be effective and let God be the one who appreciates you.

❀ ❀ ❀

Putting the Pieces Together

Make a list of the people you are currently sacrificing for. Beside each name, write how they are benefiting from your gift of time or talent. Now note why it is worth it. Most of these people may not appreciate what you are doing at this time, but God sees, God knows. So tell yourself right now, *It's worth it.*

A Positive Place

Whom do I disappoint?

alf of all children will witness the breakup of their parents' marriage. Of these, half will experience the breakup of their parents' second marriage as well.[1] By the year 2000, unwed mothers giving birth will match married women's birthrate. Half of all single mothers live below the poverty level. Girls in single-parent homes and blended families are twice as likely to drop out of school and get pregnant during their teen years.[2] The teen suicide rate has tripled in the past 30 years.[3] In 1997, 140,000 women were infected with HIV in 1997. Every six minutes a woman is raped.[4] One in four girls born will be sexually molested—70 percent by their father or the father figure of their life. One third of all children in juvenile detention centers have been sexually molested while growing up. Two million women each year are beaten by the men they live with—the majority being unmarried partners.[5]

The brokenness is overwhelming! With the world in such desperate straits, how can we "slow down"? Some people have opted for a move to rural America—but many move only to find that there are needs in those communities too! They begin serving again, cross-county from where they were. To say, "I quit!" and totally walk away isn't really an option because it isn't healthy to be a hermit. So what is a realistic option?

Salt and Light

> You are the salt of the earth. But if the salt loses its saltiness, how can it be made salty again? It is no longer good for anything, except to be thrown out and trampled by men. You are the light of the world. A city on a hill cannot be hidden (Matthew 5:13-14).

What is the responsibility of salt and light? Salt can be used for many things. Salt is a *preservative*. When meat needed preserved for a long time, it would be salted. Salt is also necessary for life preservation—people and many animals need salt to survive. On the farm I grew up on, we had salt blocks placed in important places to make sure the animals received their nutritional supplement. Salt *cleanses*. Saline solution has been used in the medical field for years for a variety of medicinal purposes. Salt is a *seasoning*. Food just tastes better—especially popcorn—when it is sprinkled with salt. Salt is a *safety tool*. When the roads and sidewalks are snowy, salt is sprinkled on them to help melt the snow and give traction to travelers. Salt helps ice melt at a cooler temperature. When you make homemade ice cream, you add salt to the ice and the ice cream freezes faster. Salt is also added to softwater heaters, to help *break down abrasive elements* in the water so our skin will feel softer and our hair will be shinier. Salt is vital!

So what does God mean when He says we are salt? Just being connected to God makes us unique. We live life differently. Our lives and values help society to be preserved. Having the Holy Spirit reside in each one of us gives the world a conscience because we have an active sense of right and wrong. We also have a God-given desire to help preserve the lives of individuals much like a nutritional supplement preserves the life of its taker. Our presence cleanses the corner of the world we live in and just being here helps wear down the corrosive evil that would run rampant if we were not here. We are a safety tool and the world doesn't usually recognize it. Our presence makes the world a better, safer, more tolerable place.

For example, have you ever thought about what would happen if you took Christ out of Christmas? There would be no gifts given because it was the wise men who brought gifts to the Babe. There would be no carols—they all talk about Jesus. There would be no tree, because it was Martin Luther who first started that tradition. There would be no stars, no angels—well it pretty much becomes empty. So it is when salt is missing, life just becomes empty.

But let's look at what salt doesn't do. Salt doesn't scream from the shaker, "Hey dummy, use me!" And it doesn't declare its worth, "Hey, did you know you couldn't walk on this sidewalk without me?" It doesn't take responsibility to go where it isn't, "Oh, wow, look there's a cut that needs to be healed, think I'll hop right over there." No, salt just stays where it is put. Salt just does its thing in its place. But salt is pretty much at home anywhere it is put and any way it is used.

Pat Clary, founder of Women's Ministry Institute, was leading a group of about 40 women leaders. To keep the conference running smoothly, she encouraged us to "stay on our side of the street." What that meant is that if we would simply stay in our area of responsibility and defer decisions outside our realm to the right person in charge of that area, life would run smoother. This is a very hard thing for women to do. We like to care about all areas. But we're just salt, sprinkled in the place God has put us—we can't be everywhere at once, only God can. Sometimes the stress that we feel is because we've picked up someone else's responsibility, someone else's territory.

This was a difficult lesson for me to learn. When my boys were just babies, I had a friend who was married to a verbally abusive man. She lived very far away from me. I gave her phone numbers, I gave her Bible study contacts, I sent her resources and told her that if things became life-threatening, she could always come stay with me until her husband obtained the counseling he needed. But I couldn't live her life. She had to follow up on the church and Bible study contacts. She had to read the resources and live out healthy boundaries and relationship principles. I couldn't rescue her. Only she could hold on to God and God would have to walk her through. I had to choose to give her problems to God and not be her god.

One day, I got a call from a prostitute. She hadn't always been a prostitute. Her husband was a successful businessman, and a mutual friend had been talking with him. He was at wit's end with his drug-abusing, runaway wife. He never really knew where she was, but his friend said he had a friend who might be able to help—me! She happened to call while my son was napping, so I took plenty of time to talk with her. She was frantic. She hadn't eaten in days. She'd sold herself the night before for drugs, and she was feeling edgy again, as if she wanted another high. She was afraid to prostitute herself again because the night before the john had become very physical and had knocked her around. I kept asking her where she was and all she kept saying was that she was in an apartment in San Diego. That didn't narrow it down much! She cried, she whined, she made no sense at times. She told me she had no clean clothes, no clean sheets and no clean towels, and bugs and rats skittered around her bed at night so she was afraid to go to sleep.

Finally I said, "If you will tell me where you are, my husband and I will come and get you and take you to a battered women's shelter where you will be safe. You can get in a drug treatment program. They have clean clothes, sheets and a warm bed and good food. I will walk you through it. Just tell me where you are."

Her response was, "Can I take my cat?"

"Honey, your cat can come with us, but it will probably have to stay at my apartment. Most shelters don't allow pets."

"If my cat can't come, then neither will I." And she hung up the phone. A faceless, downtrodden woman somewhere in San Diego called me and I had no way of finding her. I wasn't some detective or private eye. I didn't have any high tech resources available to me. All I could do was pray and trust that when she was ready, she would call again. We can be available, but we can't live people's lives for them. We're responsible *to* people, we're not responsible *for* them. We are salt. We flavor our section of the world, we cleanse our little corner of society—but we can't *make* someone use the salt shaker.

God also says we are the light of the world. A city set on a hill that cannot be hidden.

Light goes *everywhere* except where there are obstacles to its path. Turn on a light in a bedroom and the whole room is lighted, except for under the bed. Light *travels farther* when there are fewer obstacles and when there is a strong light source. The light of the sun travels much farther than the light of a single candle. Light also *warms*. The bigger the light, the warmer its glow. Light *brings life.* No light, no photosynthesis, so no plants. No plants—no food chain—no food chain—no life! Laser beams are light—focused light—and they can be used to illumine for a very great distance. Lasers can also remove obstacles. When God says we are light, He means we are *strong*! We can illumine the world so people can see God better. We bring warmth, a gentle touch to harsh humanity. We can even focus our energy and remove obstacles in our path. And we are His plan for bringing life, His life, to people.

I think that salt may represent *responsibility* and light the *authority* to carry out the responsibility. Anyone who has been in leadership knows how frustrating it is to be given a job to do and then not given the authority to make decisions to get that job done. Everything stalls and stalemates. God has clearly given us a job to do in bringing hope, healing and truth, but He's also given us the authority to carry it out.

What is our responsibility?

God's Will Made Clearer

There are only a few statements in the New Testament that clearly say, "This is God's will," or "This pleases God." I believe when we are obeying those statements, then all decisions made while obeying them become God's will. There is freedom in obeying the basic responsibilities God has laid out. Ask yourself, *am I*:

> *Saved*—This is good, and pleases God our Savior, who wants all men to be saved and to come to a knowledge of the truth (1 Timothy 2:3-4).

> *Spirit-filled*—Do not get drunk on wine, which leads to debauchery. Instead, be filled with the Spirit (Ephesians 5:18).

Sanctified—Therefore, I urge you, brothers, in view of God's mercy, to offer your bodies as living sacrifices, holy and pleasing to God—this is your spiritual act of worship. Do not conform any longer to the pattern of this world, but be transformed by the renewing of your mind. Then you will be able to test and approve what God's will is—his good, pleasing and perfect will (Romans 12:1-2).

Sexually Pure—It is God's will that you should be sanctified: that you should avoid sexual immorality (1 Thessalonians 4:3).

Saying Thanks—Give thanks in all circumstances, for this is God's will for you in Christ Jesus (1 Thessalonians 5:18).

Suffering for Right—It is better, if it is God's will, to suffer for doing good than for doing evil (1 Peter 3:17). So then, those who suffer according to God's will should commit themselves to their faithful Creator and continue to do good (1 Peter 4:19).

Seeking God—Blessed are they who keep his statutes and seek him with all their heart (Psalm 119:2). I love those who love me, and those who seek me find me (Proverbs 8:17). But if from there you seek the Lord your God, you will find him if you look for him with all your heart and with all your soul (Deuteronomy 4:29).

When I realized that all I had to do was focus on the basics and my life would please God, a new freedom settled into my heart. I could choose what to do, whom to serve and where to spend my time without spending hours worrying over the question of whether it was God's will or not. Since I knew if I simply loved God and sought Him, the rest of the list would come as a natural result, and the fretting over if I was pleasing God would be reduced to a minimum.

Pleasing People

How about people? Whom do I please, when and how often? The new question became, "Whom do I disappoint?" Because I knew I'd disappoint someone, sometime, and more likely I would disappoint a lot of someones, what would I do with all the guilt?

You will find that the more you have to give, the more people will want it from you—and the people who want it will be more and more in number. But God is very clear. You are just one person! You are *a* light. You are *a* granule of salt. You aren't an entire marquee! You aren't an entire salt mine or bag of salt. All who know Jesus are lights (though some are acting like a Bic lighter and just flicking their flame every now and again). All of us who know Jesus are small grains of salt who work together toward a common goal of preserving the world God has sprinkled us in. The world doesn't rest solely on your shoulders, even if it feels that way at times.

Jesus makes us a promise, one that seems impossible to believe: "Come to me all who are weary and heavy laden and I will give you rest. Take my yoke…and you will find rest" (Matthew 11:28-29 NKJV). Irresponsibility aside, how can we live a life that is sane and that reflects Jesus' call to rest *and* reach the world?

If it is true that you are just one person (and it is), then, as stated above, one of the key questions has to be, "Who do I disappoint and how much?" I try to function from a simple, guiding principle. Now, sometimes I have to fight my way back to it through a busy booked schedule, but I try to camp out on this principle when deciding whom to please beside God: *Some people have earned a greater right to my time.* This seems simple enough, but in reality I have found it is a difficulty for many women to discern who has more right to their time. And many women are so busy with the immediate needs of today, they can't even see the long-term ramifications of their decisions.

Who Has the Rights?

There are some relationships that are so vital, so important, that God has established their priority in Scripture. Let's look to Genesis for a peek into this principle. There were three primary relationships that God wanted fostered in the garden. Man's relationship with Him (they walked in the garden together, Genesis 3:8), the relationship between husband and wife (the two shall become one flesh, Genesis 2:24), and family (be fruitful and multiply, Genesis 1:22 and 28). When Eve listened to the serpent priorities were forever affected. And when Adam then hid with Eve instead of nurturing his relationship with God, all of humankind has borne the wounds of his decision.

Later in this book, I'll talk about how to nurture your relationship with God, so let's look now at human relationships. When God created man and woman in the garden, He instituted the priority of the family. The family is the first institution—before Israel, before the Church, before business and commerce, before community there was family. And of all the family relationships, the husband and wife relationship is preeminent.

When you stood before God and your wedding guests and said, "I do," you made a commitment to place your marriage relationship above all other relationships and responsibilities. For me, I have made a conscious choice to work on becoming an independent mate because that is what Bill needed in me as a helpmate. Being married to a man in ministry, I know that his schedule can take dramatic shifts. He can be called in on a suicide attempt, a life and death hospital call, a runaway teen or a host of "life and death" situations. I decided early on to try to keep my life and the lives of our kids as normal as possible even when the unforeseen arose. I made a choice to do fun things with friends or my children when Bill was out of town for six weeks because of youth work the summer I had a newborn. Other summers, I drove to where he was and stayed in a cabin, sometimes with friends, sometimes with just the kids. Many women would have missed out on all that fun because they wouldn't drive alone, they wouldn't drive at night or they wouldn't drive in the mountains or anywhere they haven't been before. I look at each new challenge as an adventure. An adventure to be taken as much as possible with a good attitude.

At times, this also has meant I let traditional roles fall by the wayside. For example, when I grew up, my father always packed the car for trips. But in our home, I have found we can get out of town about three hours sooner if I do all that and then simply drive by the office and pick Bill up. Since I value those three hours, I don't mind lugging a few bags to the car!

Ask your mate this question: "What things, what actions or attitudes on my part, make you feel loved and cherished?" You might be surprised at the answers.

Are there times in your day when you know that you will have your mate's undivided attention? Bill and I try to debrief and pray each night before bed. Some couples prefer to talk over coffee in the morning or a walk in the evening. Somehow, someway, you should talk each day.

Are there times in your week when you can spend a few romantic moments together? Bill and I found that we function best when we separate business and pleasure. Once a week Bill and I exercise and then have a business breakfast where we tackle issues like work responsibilities, ministry needs and family scheduling. Then one evening a week we set aside for romance. Sometimes we go out, but often we curl up for a good movie, or candlelit dinner for two, a fireside chat or an evening walk on the beach. The cost of the evening isn't important, but being together is.

But choosing to put your mate first isn't always a romantic decision. Your mate might feel most loved and respected when you stay in the family budget, or when you keep the house clean, or if you handle the kids' homework. Your mate also might feel he is playing second fiddle to a career or a school project. Most men can adapt for a once-in-awhile impending deadline push, but no one enjoys feeling like they are in second place all the time. One of my favorite proverbs is Proverbs 4:23: "Above all else, guard your heart, for it is the wellspring of life."

People go to great lengths to check their cholesterol levels because they know that if the heart is diseased, the body dies. About ten years ago, Bill and I thought we'd use a few minutes of a date to go to a free cholesterol screening. When we drove to the hospital we saw people standing in line blocks before the hospital, and they were all there for the screening. I sometimes wish there was a simple test people could take to see if their emotional heart for their spouse was diseased. It would be a healthy sign in society if there were lines of people waiting to see the results of a heart check for their love lives.

How can you tell if your heart is drifting? Each of us has some bells and whistles that should alert us that our marriage relationship is headed for trouble. Take the test below to see how your heart is doing:

1. Are you excited when his car pulls in—or out of—the driveway? (Healthy heart checks in!)

2. Do you think of ways to spend time romantically to gain more sex, or do you spend more time thinking of ways to get out of intimate encounters? (Your sex life can be a barometer of an overall healthy or unhealthy relationship.)

3. Do you enjoy talking with your husband more than your girlfriends? (You need both relationships but you should still prefer talking with your spouse.)

4. Are you still dreaming of ways to remodel the house, vacations you can take together, and places you'd like to go—someday? Or are your dreams mostly filled with scenes where you are alone or with people other than your mate?

If you answered in the negative on one, you probably just need a good vacation together. If two—it is time for a marriage conference. Three or four means counseling is in order.

For our 15th anniversary, Bill and I went on a dinner cruise around the San Diego Bay. It was so romantic: candles, soft music, lights on the water. Then the couple sitting at the table right next to ours began to talk about the bills, the kids and the IRS! Soon their conversation turned into a major argument. It was loud and caused others on the ship to become uncomfortable. Finally, the woman, in tears, said, "We can't talk like this. This is our anniversary." So they quit talking for the rest of the night! They had lost the connections!

Every year, in January, the president of the United States gives a State of the Union address, where he reviews goals and plans and prepares the country for the future. Bill and I have found it helpful to have our own *State of Our Union* meeting yearly where we talk over hopes, dreams, goals and priorities. On these weekends we discuss long-range goals (5–10 years), short-range goals (3–5 years) and immediate yearly goals. One of the questions we ask on these weekends away is: When I look back 10–20 years from now, will I think _____ was important?

There are certain seasons of life that just take more time. It is wise to ask, "What's ahead for us in the next five years?" and plan accordingly. For example, if you will be starting a family, reading books on parenthood and stabilizing your marriage and setting patterns that will prevail in romance (like date nights) will help you navigate that transition. When men and women go through mid-life transitions, they need more TLC from their spouse, so if you are married to a man who is 40–55, his mid-life needs are a consideration, as are pivotal stages like teens at home, kids in college, weddings, retirement, menopause, caring for aging parents and so on. However, if you plan ahead, life will be less likely to surprise you and you'll be prepared for the transition and will thus navigate it better.

All this is fine and dandy for married women, but what about singles? If marriage is such a big deal, how do they decide on priority relationships? After surveying my single friends, they seemed to agree on basically one thing: Spend time with those who nurture your primary relationship with God. For some, parents and siblings still held a top priority. For others, (many from non-Christian homes) they were evenly split between family and friend relationships. A key question for singles then is: "Is my relationship with God stronger or weaker after spending time with this person?"

How About the Kids?

In a survey of 1000 Christian women, Miriam Neff and Debra Kingsporn discovered that two-thirds of women work outside the home and half the women had children under age 18. One-third work because they are single women or single mothers, one-third work because their husband is either unemployed, a student or employed but in a low paying job. The final third work because they see it as part of their calling.[6]

The issue of the working v. stay-at-home mother can potentially divide women faster than anything else. However, I think it might be better if we rephrased the question altogether and asked, "What do my children need and how can I best meet those needs?" Children need different things at different ages and stages. So the question isn't "Should I work or not" but "How can I best meet the needs of my children?"

Science has also shown that children gain more confidence and security later in life if they have bonded to one primary infant caretaker.[7] So the question isn't, "Do I work?" but rather, "How can I become a primary caretaker? How can I ensure a stable beginning and a secure bonding with this child I brought into this world?" When I was pregnant, I was overwhelmed with the amount of information I read encouraging me to nurse because infants get a stronger start physically and emotionally when mom nurses.

Toddlers and preschoolers have a need for a safe environment, freedom to learn and a smaller social circle. Selma Frailberg, while a professor at the University of Michigan, discovered that children under three fared best when cared for by mother, and those three to six could sustain absence from mother for half a day, but didn't tolerate well a prolonged absence of ten to twelve hours.[8] The question then becomes, "How can I best see that these needs are met?"

Living with toddlers might mean you change your attitude about what constitutes a "clean" house. You might find yourself reprioritizing. I remember my middle child being very inquisitive and wanting everyone to see everything he saw. Often he said, "Mom, come here." My standard reply was, "Just a minute, honey." Once I walked out after a couple, "just a minute honey's" and said, "Whatcha need, Zach?"

"Never mind, the beautiful butterfly flew away. It's too late. It's always too late."

And he was right, I'd been putting him off more and more. Since we were working in youth ministry at the time, I was reminded that there might come a day when he would no longer want me intricately involved in his life. The more I put him off now, the sooner that day would come because children can sense when you are not interested. I made a conscious choice that day that, as much as possible, I'd come when called to share some exciting moment, because the moments would be over all too soon.

School-age children need a strong education, so each year Bill and I ask, "What is best for this child—homeschool, private school or public school?" The answer to this question may change with each child, geographic location or a variety of other variables like spotting a child's giftedness and providing opportunities for growth in those areas. School-age children need support to grow and develop an identity, so it's important to address the question of "How will we as a family make sure each child feels supported and their talents and giftedness nurtured?"

Teens need time, lots and lots of time, for you to listen to them as they talk out their value system. Most teens also need some space to fine-tune their giftedness and to have time and opportunities to hear God's calling on their lives for decisions like romance, vocation, morality. Ask yourself, "How can I be that listening ear, that sounding board and the source of opportunity to fine-tune their call? Or do I need to cover other family needs so my husband can be more available to the teens?"

Add to these questions the issues of finances. "What does my child truly *need* v. what is a *want*?" In the 20 years Bill and I have been in ministry, we have seen great kids come from homes where mom is home full-time, where she works from the home and where she works part-time or full-time away from home. And the opposite is also true. We've seen kids who are a mess who are launched from all four environments. So whether to work or not work isn't the right question, again the question is, *"Is my heart turned toward home?"*

Are you learning about developmental stages and do you know your children well enough to spot changes in stages and changes in character? There is much wisdom in listening to those who have already been there. As a young mother, I was constantly told:

- Spend time with your children while they are young and they will want to spend time with you when they get older. They will want to spend time with you even when their peers aren't spending time with family.

- They grow up fast. Cherish those early years.

- You don't want to miss those first steps and those first words.

- The preschool years are foundational. One mother told me, "How they act at 4 is how they will act at 14—only they will be bigger and you can't carry them to their room anymore!" (And I think she was right—so far two of mine have passed into their teen years and their basic temperament is similar to their obedience level and temperament at 4!)

- Pay now or pay later. That was advice I received about early discipline. And I am glad I spent extra time—and I mean *extra*, in correcting attitudes and behaviors in the toddler preschool years. My teen boys treat me with respect and they are pretty responsible and helpful when many moms of teens feel very abandoned, fearful and dumped on. While I have been writing this book, my fourteen-year-old has started public high school, and in just a few short months he has been named Football Offensive Player of the Year. He was named scholar athlete with the highest GPA on the team (a tie with one other at 4.17), he has been inducted into the Blue Pride Club, a recognition that is only given when a teacher recommends a student to the Associated Student Body officers, who then vote (two teachers recommended Brock). He has hosted a team outreach pizza party where 45 players came and 26 received Christ and has helped launch a Bible study for those athletes. The best part is that he treats his mom, dad, friends and teachers with respect. Investing early will raise the possibility of dividends later.

Patrick Morley says in *The Man in the Mirror*, "Set your priorities by who will cry at your funeral." This one really helps if you run your own business or work in ministry. Because Bill's job description includes a large number of funerals, I've really noticed who comes: family! They will fly, drive or walk if necessary to get to the graveside. The next group that will be there are close friends. These people may have started out as clients, parishioners, community friends or neighbors, but somewhere along the line a loyalty was built and you can see signs of that loyalty in your life's crisis points. Who calls to check if you're emotionally okay? Who comes to your side in a crisis? Who lends a helping hand during rough financial, emotional or career stages?

Another question I ask is, "Who have I chosen to commit myself to?" These people also get a higher priority on my time. For example, if I commit to a discipleship or mentoring relationship, those people gain an inside track so they can reach me easier. Colleagues in business and ministry with whom I have formed some kind of an alliance get their calls returned first.

I also ask, "Who has paid the price to have access to me?" My mother gained that right when she walked the floors with me on sleepless nights. My sister did when she befriended me when I didn't have any friends. My brother did when he protected me growing up. My mentors did when they gave me much-needed advice or a foot in the door. Those who have worked tirelessly alongside me in ministry year after year, either with time or money, gain a greater degree of access.

Yes, we want to help meet needs but the need is not the call. Just because someone has spent a lifetime making poor choices and living contrary to God's plan doesn't mean you have to run to "fix" their life when they are feeling the stress of those choices. If we rescue too early, those people may never have to depend on God because they have us. They may also never experience the pain of their consequences, so they then make the same bad decisions over and over because they know you'll come running to the rescue.

So my next question I ask myself is, "Are my actions and behaviors toward others maintaining my integrity and character?" I never want to be flippant when people are in need, but I also don't always have to be the one who meets the need. Just because I am busy doesn't mean I want my standards to drop personally or professionally. When I see myself cutting corners, these become yellow caution lights and I reevaluate. When I start not wanting people to stop by because the house is a mess, or when I feel people have received second best, I reevaluate, regroup, reprioritize and redelegate.

I ask, "Am I reflecting the character of God?" Several years ago, I was going out of town and someone called wanting information and books on our ministry. I frantically ran around, arranging how to get the bookstore items they wanted, how and when we might speak, and a variety of other things. Later on the plane, I asked myself, "Why did I think that couldn't wait five days?" Now some things can't wait five days, but in this instance it could have waited two weeks and it wouldn't have changed anything! The verse, "For God is not a God of disorder but of peace" (1 Corinthians 14:33) flipped into my mind. I tried to picture God frantically running around heaven shoving blessings into FedEx boxes and the picture just didn't fit! So now I ask, "What are the consequences if this isn't done this minute? Today? Tomorrow? This week? This month? This year!" I then prioritize with long-range consequences in mind and not just by adrenaline or the squeaky wheel.

I sometimes ask, "If I don't meet this need is there a ministry, resource or institution that is already in place that can meet the need?" Most often the answer is yes! So I try not to reinvent wheels.

"Am I doing now what will buy me time later?" That's the reason I taught the kids to be a part of the team in keeping the house clean. Yes, maybe those preschoolers and early elementary years were filled with lumpy beds that they'd made and half-swept floors, but now it warms my heart to see the boys taking charge of chores like laundry, the garage, dishes and so on. Because all my boys have had chores nearly their entire lives, we all have more time functioning as a team and it's not only mom doing everything and the family watching and waiting. This meant I had to give up my ownership and that I had to trust my husband and children to accomplish the same task but in their own way.

When you've asked all the questions and it's still not clear, then what? A couple of years ago, all my boys had something important on the same night. One son had an awards' ceremony, another an all-star team meeting and the third a ball game. They each thought their event should bring mom out—and of course they were in three different places at the exact same time. (This is now a very normal occurrence!) The more children you have the more this will happen. The more commitments you've made, the more likely the schedule will double and triple booking will happen. So what do you do on days when all the options seem like "A" priorities?

Pray. It may sound simplistic, but on those difficult scheduling decisions, when I've prayed one option usually rises to the surface or sometimes creative alternatives take place. My biggest questions are usually, "What is the worst thing that will happen if I'm not there?" "What is the worst thing that can happen if I don't get this done?" A child might feel slighted—not a big thing unless the child senses there is a pattern of him or her getting the short end of the scheduling stick. Maybe it is a missed opportunity. Usually it will not be something that is once-in-a-lifetime—but sometimes it is. There will only be one time a daughter is crowned homecoming queen, one wedding (hopefully!), one graduation of eighth grade, high school and college. On those days the decisions seem clear, but they aren't always.

I was at the Chosen Women stadium event for women where Anne Lotz had been scheduled to speak a year or more ahead. That evening she brought her daughter to the podium and introduced her to the nearly 35,000 women gathered. It seems she and her daughter had a scheduling dilemma to solve. Mom was scheduled to speak the same night her daughter was to graduate from Baylor University. As they shared how they had prayed and weighed out the discussion, the entire stadium rose to their feet and gave the daughter a standing ovation. Her graduation would have been memorable—no doubt—but not as memorable as a stadium packed with women standing to their feet spontaneously and giving *her* a standing ovation!

The principle I saw displayed that night was the teamwork principle. On those tough scheduling days, I bring in back up. I ask my husband's opinion, or sometimes my children's. If it is a ministry conflict, I'll ask the people involved. By knowing more of what is planned for the event or meeting, you can often gain the necessary information to make a decision. I don't ask my children when they are very young (the burden is too adult for them) but as my children enter their preteen years, I begin to pull them in on family scheduling decisions. I check in with the boys often to see how they think their "mom time" is going.

Recently my oldest said, "Mom, don't get me wrong. I'm glad you care and you ask me, but don't get paranoid. I know you have to miss some of my games to keep shoes on these feet and your money sends me to sports camps. I'm not going to grow up and be all dysfunctional and write a my-mom-was-a-committed-Christian-leader-so-I'm-dysfunctional book. If I turn out dysfunctional, it will be because I chose wrong decisions. Mom, I'm a leader because you showed me how to be bossy and still love people like you do" (I *think* that was a compliment!)

When talking over some life choices with Fern Nichols, the founder of *Moms in Touch,* she said something to me I'll never forget. "Pam, sometimes it is the right thing, but the wrong time." There is so much freedom in that one statement. We often feel moved and want to respond when we hear about social issues like abortion, child abuse, teen pregnancy, the homeless and a myriad of other opportunities in our community, country or the world. It is at those times I reflect on the timing. I ask myself, "Is this the right time or could I do this later in my life?" After my children leave home, I have an "A.K." list (After Kids) that has things on it such as: Take up photography, learn to watercolor, use my leadership skills for the pro-life movement, volunteer for political campaign office work, create a women's center to meet needs of women in transition (single mothers, launchers of home businesses, stay-at-home mothers, returning students, women who want off welfare, women getting out of prison, and so on). These are all good things, and in the past I have participated in many of them but right now, because of the age of my children, my activity in these areas is very limited.

So What Do I Do with the Guilt?

You know the feeling. It's the pit in your stomach. It's the cloud hanging over your head. The sinking, shrinking, stinking feeling of wanting to run away, avoid, cocoon so we won't have to face the person who we think is disappointed in us. It is that "waiting for the other shoe to drop" foreboding that resembles the suspenseful music at the crescendo of a thriller movie. You wonder what price you'll have to pay the piper for going against the status quo. You question over and over in your mind if you made the right decision. Your chest tightens, your sleep is fitful and your head feels as though it's in a vise. You wonder if the gauge on the blood pressure cuff would explode if it took your pulse. This is guilt.

How can you tell where the feeling of guilt is coming from? How can you tell if it is conviction from the Holy Spirit, which you do want to listen to, or guilt from Satan, which you don't want to listen to?

Satan will:

Condemn. He will accuse and replay the accusations until you feel like a prisoner on death row. The Bible is clear that "there is now no condemnation for those who are in Christ Jesus" (Romans 8:1). Condemnation is adverse judgment, strong disapproval or the results of being judged unfit. It is that nagging, gnawing feeling that you don't measure up to some arbitrary standard and you never will. You're stuck in life, flailing in the quicksand of public opinion or at least in the opinion of someone.

Confuse. The Bible points out that God is not the God of disorder. When Satan plays with your mind, he doesn't play fair. He will toss out all kinds of half-truths, partial proposals, and a host of conflicting statements. His goal is to distract you and make you so preoccupied that you can't move forward in your calling. He wants you self-absorbed and he'll throw out distortions and misconceptions in rapid-fire motion to keep you caught up like a deer in the headlights. Satan's accusations will make you paralyzed, immobile and stunned in self-doubt.

Cause your heart to become calloused. Satan's accusations will make you overreact. You'll hear yourself say things like, "Who cares!" "I give up, anyway!" "Why try?" "Whatever!" Your goal in life will become selfish protectionism. You'll go from healthy boundaries to a walled-in fortress protecting you from all emotions, not just bad, but good emotions also. When your defensive walls go up, everyone and everything will be kept at bay, not just the people who make you feel bad, but everyone.

Connive you into over-compensation. Satan will drive you until you take responsibility that isn't yours. He will whisper lies to you until you feel indispensable, irreplaceable, and like a lone ranger. You'll hear yourself saying, "I'm the only one! If I don't do it, no one will!" You'll fall headlong into the martyr role. You will stomp around the house showing everyone you are the one doing all the work. You'll proclaim your martyrdom to anyone who will listen. "I was the only one here last night. I stayed until 4 A.M. All I did was shower and change. I didn't get any sleep."

Jesus and the Holy Spirit will:

Be consistent. His promptings will always be in line with His Word. His prompting will also be the same or similar day after day. For example, I remember God wanting to address my short fuse. I would turn on the radio and the preacher would talk about anger. I would pick up magazines and find articles on anger. I even yelled up the stairs to my sons to quit yelling and Caleb, the youngest, said, "Mom, I don't think God likes it when you yell." *Okay, God, I get the message!*

Be positive. The correction and conviction of the Holy Spirit may be strong but it is always stated in positive terms. God may point out that an action or attitude is wrong, but He won't call you stupid or bombard you with thoughts of how useless and irredeemable you are.

Be forward thinking. The Spirit will most likely point out "why" a decision was wrong or incomplete. God will remind you of long-term consequences, long-range goals, and eternal values. His conviction will force you to think things through and think things out in an orderly fashion, keeping the end result in view. God will take you to the finish line and walk you back through the race so you can run it better.

Be specific. Instead of vague innuendoes, God will tell you exactly what to correct. He won't say, "Wow, you should feel really bad about yesterday." He will say things like, "Just now, the words you used to talk to Bill were really cutting and sarcastic. Do you want to hurt him like that? Look at his face. Put yourself in his place."

The first time I met Carina I could tell she was depressed. She was slumped over in her chair, weepy, and she had visible signs of stress: a flush on her neck, a rash on her forearm, nails bitten to the quick. The more Carina talked, the more I could see why she was stressed. She wasn't just carrying her own stress of being a single mother trying to provide for her child, but she was carrying her entire family's struggles and personally feeling responsible for six other adults (her parents, a grandparent and three siblings). All the adults in her family were either sick, broke, on drugs, or in trouble with the law or had a marriage on the rocks! These adults expected Carina to clean not only her house, but her parents', her grandmother's and a couple of sibling's homes as well, and each of those adults were healthier physically than Carina was! I was sitting across from a modern day Cinderella!

As a little girl, I loved that fairy tale. Cinderella was a beautiful young woman who had the misfortune of having her mother pass away and her father remarry an evil woman. When her father died, her stepmother and stepsisters treated her cruelly—like a lowly servant. Fortunately, one day her Fairy Godmother flew into Cinderella's life and created a lovely ball gown and provided a horse and carriage out of a set of mice and a pumpkin!

There's No Fairy Godmother, Baby!

Many women today are living the first part of the Cinderella story. We are carrying burdens and responsibilities that God didn't design for us to carry. In our hearts, we cry out, hoping that a fairy godmother will swoop down and rescue us, but God didn't create life to be lived out waiting for someone else to intervene and change our lives. He wants us to take responsibility for our own life changes.

Freedom from guilt will not come from a fairy godmother, or from someone coming in and flippantly saying, "It's okay, forget it." Freedom from guilt will only come as we learn to discern God's voice from Satan's. "Guilt was intended to drive us to the cross where we will experience forgiveness and freedom."[9] As you sort through the expectations that everyone has about you and your life, remember that healthy boundaries will send you back toward God. He will remind you: You are salt—*one* grain. You are light—*a* light! A woman knows her place in His plan when she knows she is limited and only God is limitless.

Putting the Pieces Together

Pray through the description of how God leads. Now make a list of the people in your life that have earned more right to your time. Brainstorm ways to keep them a higher priority. Now talk to a trusted friend and share when you are most vulnerable to guilt sent from Satan. See if you can recognize some of his common lies that he uses to make you feel guilty and defeated.

The Resting Place

What do I do when I'm sick and tired of being sick and tired?

You drag yourself in the door. Your arms are loaded with more work than you feel you can possibly ever get done, so you drop the burden of books, papers, briefcases, files and bags in the middle of the floor. You don't even bother to turn on the light because you don't want to look at the state the house is in. You're not sure if you want to take a long, hot bath or just skip it all together and collapse on your bed fully dressed. You're hungry but making anything seems like such a bother. Your head is pounding, your heart is racing and your body aches. You are sick of coffee, sick of people, sick of the demands and sick of life. You want to just curl up in a little ball and lock all the doors, unplug all the phones, pagers, faxes and emails, but even that seems like work. You simply lean against the wall and slide down, collapsing in a heap on the floor. Your head buries itself in your knees and you wrap your arms around yourself because you could really use a hug. You aren't sure if you want to live or die and you don't care, because thinking hurts. You want to cry, but you're even too tired to feel.

Stress and Burnout

In his book *Living the Life You Were Meant to Live,* Tom Peterson notes:

> People often come to me complaining of burnout. I point out to them that they may be approaching burnout, but they have not yet experienced it. The person who truly becomes burned out has undergone an irreversible change...I have often counseled top executives about employees under their supervision, "You allowed this person to reach the point of burnout. You were insensitive to his needs and to where he was at in approaching burnout. Now it is time to deal sensitively with how you are going to reposition that person."

> Executives frequently respond, "I'll give him time off— several months if need be. That should refresh him."

> "No," I advise. "The person has burned out. That particular light cannot be lit again. He has no more value to you, or to himself, in that position or in that department. Find a new area for him. Find a replacement for his old position. The person's talents remain, but he has lost all

motivation for doing his old job and he'll never be able to regain it. *Burnout is irreversible.*"[1] (Emphasis mine.)

Dr. Archibald Hart in an interview with Focus on the Family explained the difference between stress and burnout as stress being primarily biological and burnout being more emotional. Dr. Hart sees stress as "running in emergency mode." The body uses too much adrenaline, the cholesterol goes up, blood pressure goes up, the heart pounds, the hands get cold. And the result is accelerated wear and tear on the body. Depression can result, but it is the result of physical exhaustion.

On the other hand, burnout is an emotional response that produces demoralization often resulting from feeling a lack of affirmation, depleted resources and no support system to help you cope. There is a lack of vision and an "I don't care" attitude that develops.[2]

Dr. Hart explains that burnout sneaks up on us. "Our bodies can adapt to circumstances that in the long run are hard on us—such as when we carry too much stress for too long a period of time. After awhile we get so used to it, we no longer recognize it for what it really is—distress."[3]

Dr. Kwang Ja Park, Director of Missionary Mobilization for Overseas Crusades, sees burnout as a preventable problem in a woman's life. "I see so many leaders, even ones in their 20s and 30s, so tired. They cry a lot. And ones in menopause, they are so tired and cry, I never experienced that." Dr. Park's secret was discovered several years into ministry. In Korea, she was a part of a seminary class of 300 men and two women who headed out to full-time vocational ministry. After she had been serving as a missionary in the jungles of the Amazon for eight years, she came home on a furlough and picked up a book by a leading pastor at that time. "I don't remember the title, or page number, but I remember one sentence, 'You need two separate goals: ministry goals *and* personal goals.'" She put the book down and registered at Fuller Seminary, not because she needed anymore diplomas but because learning replenishes her soul.

"All this go, go, go, go and do, do, do, do. We become no different than those in business just trying to get ahead. But for the Lord's workers, spiritual growth and personal maturity are so important."[4]

At her graduation from Fuller, she was asked to give a message to her classmates. The message was her life. "Do something for yourself, for your growth and you will never burn out in ministry." She had experienced the principle firsthand. As the first Korean woman to hold a full-time church staff position as a Christian Education Director at Young Nak Presbyterian Church, Dr. Park saw the church grow from 600 to 8,000 in sixteen years—and the first ten of those she was in seminary. She went on her days off to reenergize her own life, "Those goals revitalized me." For 58 years Dr. Park has laid down her life in service for God, and she is still fresh and growing.

Pursuing R and R

The principle of regular rest is built into the Old Testament. God instructed that one day in seven be for rest, a Sabbath. You weren't supposed to work, travel, have people work for you or cook—but you were to rest in God. You were to focus on how good He'd been to you. Each year in Israel there were approximately 70 days of festivals. With the Sabbaths and celebrations the Israelites received approximately 120 days off a year. Then God set aside one year in seven for the land to rest. There was to be no planting or harvesting—so the farmers got the year off too.

Once every 50 years, there was a Year of Jubilee. In this year there was no sowing or harvesting. During this year all were to return their home property to their clan. Indentured servants were freed and debts forgiven. While life didn't come to a complete standstill in the seventh-year Sabbaths or in the Year of Jubilee, life was dramatically altered. Most people didn't work. Families were reunited. They were years of reflection, regrouping and transitioning.

God has also built rest into individual lives. In Israel's tradition, soldiers didn't have to serve in the army the first year after they were married. Are you building Sabbath rests, celebration and jubilee into your own life? Educators receive sabbaticals to study and rest so they have more to give out when they return. Are you any different? Don't you feel like you give and give and give? Everyone needs time to reflect, regroup and receive from God so they can be reenergized for life.

What revitalizes you? Is there a gift you can give yourself that will build into you as a person? Most women have grand hopes and dreams for ministry. They have ambitious plans for their children and family, but do you have a satisfying plan for you, one that will develop your inner person? Give yourself a gift—rather, allow God to give you the gift He has that is waiting to replenish you.

The Gift of Emotional Connection

There are certain behaviors that rebuild and replenish us to give us the ability to go on. It seems even the scientific community has discovered the truth that the Bible has long proposed, "...and the greatest of these is love" (1 Corinthians 13:13). A variety of professionals in the fields of psychology, medicine and psychiatry are writing on the connection between the giving and receiving of love and good health. In a study at Yale University, scientists studied 119 men and 40 women who were undergoing treatment for coronary angiography. Those patients who felt most loved and supported had substantially less blockage.[5]

Over 700 elderly adults were studied for the affects of aging. The researchers concluded the lack of degeneration had more to do with what the participants *contributed* to their social support network than what they received from it. The more love and support they offered, the more they benefited from it themselves.[6] In a study of nearly 3,000 men and women for a duration of nine to twelve years, those that volunteered to help others once a week were two and a half times less likely to die during the course of the study as those who did not volunteer.[7] (So my mom was right, it is what you give, not what you get, that is important!)

Emotional connections early in life seem to affect our health later in life. In a 35-year follow-up study out of Harvard, 91 percent of participants in one study that didn't perceive themselves as having a warm relationship with their mother growing up were diagnosed with serious diseases in midlife. Only 45 percent of those who described their relationship with mom as nurturing became ill. In the same way, 82 percent who ranked their relationship with dad as low in emotional warmth were diagnosed with severe diseases by midlife as compared to 50 percent who ranked their relationship with their father as warm and close. If the participants rated their relationship with *both* mom and dad as low in warmth, 100 percent had been diagnosed with a disease by midlife.[8] (This kind of makes you want to pick up the phone and reach out and touch someone you love, doesn't it?!)

In a study of post-surgical patients, those who lacked regular participation in an organized social group were four times as likely to be dead six months after surgery. Those who had *no* religious affiliation from which they gained comfort and strength were three times as likely to be dead in six months and those who had *neither* a religious or social support network were seven times as likely to be dead within six months.[9] (Now here's some new motivation to get up and out of bed and get to church on Sunday mornings, right?)

In a study of women with breast cancer, one group received the traditional treatment of radiation, chemotherapy and surgery and the other received the same treatment plus a 90-minutes per week group session with other cancer survivors for one year. As the women were tracked, the weight of the study showed that those who met in that group for the first year following cancer treatment lived twice as long as those who did not! And all those women who were not a part of the follow-up support group were all dead within five years.[10]

One specialist in this area of science concluded that:

> The more friends you have, the healthier you are. However, this effect is due, almost exclusively, to the degree which you have talked with your friends about any traumas that you have suffered. But here's the kicker. If you have had trauma that you have not talked about with anyone, the number of friends you have is unrelated to your health. (Social support only protects your health if you use it wisely.)[11]

Dr. Dean Ornish, a leader in the field of treatment of heart patients and prevention of heart disease, was himself struggling with some life choices about career opportunities that were presenting themselves. His friend said to him, "If you are swimming in an ocean and someone offers you a big bag of gold—a golden opportunity—if you take that bag and hold on to it, you will drown. Are you going to hold on to something that will keep you from what most nourishes your soul? Either you let go now or you become a slave to the very thing you created and it tells you how to live."

Reflecting on this conversation, Dr. Ornish writes: "When my self-worth was defined by what I did, then I had to take every important opportunity that came along, even if a relationship suffered. Now I understand that *real power is measured not by how much you have but by how much you can walk away from."* (Emphasis mine.)[12]

This decision to allow yourself to be emotionally connected is a daily one. Those who are task-oriented individuals, like myself, may struggle with it most. One particularly hectic day, I was at my desk trying to cram as much as possible into my schedule before I had to pick up my children at school at 2:30. I was racing the clock and I picked up the phone and dialed, then looked at my watch—2:30. The face of my precious eight-year-old flashed across my mind. At that moment I knew that the tentacles of the *To Do List* had wrapped its strong claws into my heart and the only way to deal with it was with some quick machete action to my heart. My kids matter more. I hung up the phone, pushed myself away from my desk in my rolling office chair and said out loud with conviction: *Pam, walk away. Just walk away!*

Hugs matter. That day they mattered even more because the loving arms of my eight-year-old son reminded me of what is important. Meaningful work is important, but emotional connection is more important. Now it is easier to give myself permission to just *walk away, walk away, walk away—and walk to the arms of someone I have committed to love.*

The Gift of Contentment

Meyer Friedman, the doctor who pioneered the concept of the Type-A personality, pinpointed some research in the area of Type A behaviors. It was first thought that just being a Type-A driving, go get' em personality made you a greater risk for heart disease, but it was found that only those with one particular component or trait were at high risk—hostility! So it's not moving at a quick clip that is the problem as much as your attitude while doing it!

Dr. Archibald Hart agrees:

Emotional upsets such as fear, anxiety, depression and anger can be shown to raise both adrenaline and cholesterol levels....As far as personality characteristics are concerned, two "dimensions" have been found to be associated with elevated cholesterol:

-*overactivity* (excessive competition, aggression, and impatience)

-*overcontrol* (exaggerated sense of responsibility, conformism, and low self-esteem)

Both of these personality traits are associated with the Type-A behavior pattern, which is known also to produce higher levels of adrenaline. Another psychological factor contributing to the recruitment of cholesterol appears to be that of "perceived helplessness"...when a person is caught up in a situation about which he or she feels helpless and has no control over the outcome, cholesterol as well as adrenaline levels increase significantly...There is only one way to diet or exercise in a healthy, stress-lowering manner, and that is to avoid frustration, over-competitiveness, and hostility while you're doing it.[13]

In treating heart attack patients, Dr. Friedman saw the most striking success at prevention of a reoccurring heart attack was to place patients in a supportive small group environment. The doctor explains, "Perhaps more than any other thing a leader can do for these patients is to provide them with what many did not adequately secure in childhood—unconditional love and affection from a respected parent figure."[14]

Are you emotionally connected? Are you giving your life away to those younger in age, younger in spiritual growth or others? Are you allowing your schedule to reflect your own need for emotional connection? Where do you receive love?

The Gift of Physical Care

The best gift of encouragement I received was from a colleague who helps busy professionals in ministry take care of themselves. Dr. Earl Henslin told me to picture the gift of exercise in a way that I would be motivated to receive it. He then gave an example of a person who calculated how much productivity was gained by exercising one hour a day. For example, if exercising one hour a day will help you be able to work an extra hour, then you've gained an hour's worth of wages. Or if exercising one hour makes you more creative, then you've gained the positive outcome of the additional creativity, and if exercising an hour everyday will help you live longer, then you've gained years of productivity and those years can be spent however you and God deem worthy.

For me, having a way to measure the worth of an hour of my productivity renewed my motivation. In my family history, heart disease runs rampant. My father has nine siblings—and most of them had their first signs of heart problems before the age of 35! One brother died at 36, and several more in their late 50s and early 60s. Nearly all of them have had heart surgery.

Motivation to live has been a very real working motivation for me to exercise at least some everyday. I tell myself, "You will die if you do not work out today." I know God made my body to function under certain health principles and if I follow them, things work better. I love the test Daniel threw out to the king's officials in Daniel 1. Daniel wanted healthy fruits and vegetables rather than the rich food from the king's table, so he asked the official to test his health against those who ate off the king's table. After ten days Daniel and his buddies' "appearance seemed better …than all the youths who had been eating the king's choice food" (Daniel 1:15 NASB).

So test the system. Some people are motivated when they can calculate the monetary value of a workout. For example, if a business owner or a woman working on commission is earning $50,000 a year, she is averaging about $20 per hour. The benefit of working out is that she is more alert and clear thinking, so she can accomplish an extra hour's worth of work in the same amount of time, and now she's ahead $20 more a day. If a membership to a workout gym is costing her $1 per day, then each workday she will now earn $19 more because of the added time and productivity. If there are twenty working days in the month, she will earn $380 more per month or $4,560 more per year.

If she is 35 when she makes this decision, then she'll earn $136,800 more by the age of 65 than a woman who does not work out. If you add in the fact that she will probably live longer, let's say 10 years longer than the average woman, she could earn almost $550,000 more in her lifetime if she works during those extra 10 years. Add these two numbers together and she would wind up with added earning potential of $687,000 over her lifetime by paying $9,600 for a gym membership. Working out could net her $677,400. The $20 a month health club membership doesn't look as expensive when you look at its potential returns.

I know that money should not be our prime motive in life. But I also know that women, by and large, tend to not value themselves or their time. By looking at the long-term consequences of a decision, through a variety of models, you can sometimes gain a clearer picture of the intangible value of a choice.

If you add to this paradigm the next lens of longevity, meaning that you can personally be healthy enough to actively be involved in your grandchildren's lives, or extend your ministry to the next generation, then the positives of disciplining your life to exercise regularly becomes a higher priority.

Dr. Michael Roizen, professor of Medicine and Chair of the Department of Anesthesia and Critical Care at the Pritzer School of Medicine at the University of Chicago, wrote a book called

RealAge: Are You as Young as You Could Be? Dr. Roizen explained the concept of *RealAge* to me:

> *RealAge* is a scientifically valid measure of how fast your body is aging. *RealAge* is different from your calendar age, which is simply the number of birthdays you have had; your *RealAge* tells exactly how fast you are aging. For example, I am 53 calendar years of age, but my *RealAge* is 38. The *RealAge* book tells us 44 steps that have been scientifically proven to retard or reverse aging, and how much each of those steps changes your *RealAge*. I like to think of *RealAge* as a Currency for Health. If I gave you $50, you would know that you could get your haircut or buy dinner, but you wouldn't have enough money for a house, and you would have too much for a cup of coffee. That is the potential of money; that is, it lets us value our choices and make decisions that are rational for us. *RealAge* is like money in that it values our choices. None of us will do everything, but *RealAge* lets us know what each factor does to our age so we can make choices that are rational for us.

Dr. Roizen thinks even busy women have options. He says, "Everyone has to make their own choices. What is doable for one woman is difficult for another. Finding out your *RealAge* and choosing what you want to do to make your *RealAge* younger takes just 30 to 40 minutes. And it's fun. And you'll learn how you can gain that 30 minutes back many times over by becoming younger. After analyzing the factors, you can choose to do things that appeal to you to make you younger. Virtually every woman can retard her aging. The program will offer each person specific achievable recommendations."[15]

Dana Demetre, a nurse and health care professional who authored *The LifeStyle Dimensions Program* encourages women to balance their lives physically, mentally, emotionally and spiritually. She encourages women to take small steps back to health.

Instead of dieting, Demetre encourages women to think active. "We think our sedentary lifestyle is normal because it is all we know. The average American woman only burns between 1,500 and 1,800 calories each day. However, in the early 1900s, she burned between 2,000 and 3,000 each day!...People walked everywhere and engaged in physical labor everyday...In order to make long-term change and stay lean for life, you must make a lifestyle change that includes increased activity."[16]

One of the changes I have recently made is to make walking dates instead of coffee dates for those women who are wanting appointments for emotional issues or leaders whom I need to touch base with. Most of the women are very receptive because they are also struggling with how to fit more activity into their lives as well.

Even drinking more water will help most women. We should drink four to eight ounces of water every hour. If you're awake from 7 A.M. until 11 P.M. then that's about 64 to 128 ounces a day or more than two quarts of water a day minimum. Here's the catch, coffee or cola doesn't count; in fact, for every ounce of caffeine you drink, you need to drink an exra ounce of water! Caffeine is a diuretic, so it depletes your body of the much-needed water.[17]

Don't be dismayed. "Small steps, taken consistently, add up in a big way over time," says Demetre.[18]

When we show care for ourselves, we reflect the character of God. God cares for us. He says "You are *the temple of the Holy Spirit*" (1 Corinthians 6:19). You are *God's temple* (1 Corinthians 3:16). This means our bodies house the Creator who made them. You became His temple the moment you received Christ into your life.

If God sent me an announcement that He was coming to visit my house, I'd mobilize my whole family into action. Closets and drawers would get emptied and organized. We'd dust, mop, scrub, vacuum and even do the windows and clean out the garage! I'd go into action to get everything ready for His visit, but He isn't visiting—He already lives here. Because He is always around, I forget how important it is to take care of His place—me! God wants me to look at all my habits and health practices in light of His view of me—a temple. A palace that is holy, houses the truth and proclaims the good news of love, joy, peace, patience, kindness, goodness, gentleness, faithfulness and self-control (Galatians 5:22-23).

Since God interconnected our body, our emotions and our spirit, when one responds positively to His plan, all the other areas are affected positively too. The psalmist relays this connection in an example from Psalm 30:10-12: "Hear, O LORD, and be merciful to me; O LORD, be my help. [A cry for emotional help.] You turned my wailing into dancing; [emotional help came, so there is a positive physical response] you removed my sackcloth and clothed me with joy, [a recap of the emotional help that was received] that my heart may sing to you and not be silent. O LORD my God, I will give you thanks forever [positive spiritual result occurred]." Enjoying the gift of physical health can help you spiritually as well.

The Gift of Prayer

A church decided to test the power of prayer on evangelism. Eighty names were chosen out of the phone book and the church prayed for them for three months. At the same time 80 more names were chosen from the phone book, but this group received no prayer. At the end of the three months, both groups were phoned by church members. Of the 80 who had received no prayer only one responded favorably, but out of the group that had been prayed for, 69 invited church members to visit and 45 even invited the church prayer teams in for coffee, refreshments—and a time of prayer![19]

Medical science has even linked the power of prayer to patient longevity and recovery. Dr. Dale A. Matthews of Georgetown University reviewed 212 studies and found that three-fourths showed a positive correlation between religious commitment and good health. In a San Francisco study, 393 patients were divided into two groups. Half were prayed for and half were not. No one knew which group they were placed in. Those who were prayer recipients had fewer health complications.[20]

If prayer is so good for others and us, then why is it so hard to accomplish? I think it is because we look at prayer as a task rather than a relationship. Prayer isn't something I do, it is Someone I talk to. For me, prayer is best when I am able to be myself while talking to God. A few things have helped me nurture this relationship.

Know whom I'm talking to. The more I have learned about God, His character and personality, the more I want to talk to Him. I have studied the names of God, the names of Jesus and the names of the Holy Spirit. I have done studies on the attributes of God and I have dug into inductive Bible studies to see how God works with and through people. As I experience God, I gain motivation to pray because I realize over and over what an awesome privilege it is. I have a building confidence that talking with Him will make a difference in my life. When I reflect on His sovereignty and omniscience, that He sees everything, knows everything and has all power to do anything He sees best, my struggles seem safer in His hands. It is when I stop spending time getting to know Him through Bible study that I wane in my motivation to meet Him.

Know it is okay to be real. Great freedom comes in knowing that God knows everything about me and loves me in spite of myself.

For nearly twenty years, Bill and I have enjoyed praying while being real and vulnerable before God. When we pray, if our mind wanders, we simply start praying about that area of life. We assume that because our mind went there, it is either an issue we need to address—or one God wants us to examine. For example, I might start out praying for one of my boys, but then my mind jumps to a work deadline. I'll pray through that issue until I feel peace or release from its burden. Then I'll go back to praying for my son. I will even pray through sinful thoughts as they come. If I'm trying to focus on God and His attributes but a scene from TV, some obnoxious commercial or cruel thought comes into my mind, I'll pray and commit that area to God. I'll confess that it is wrong, then ask God to take my thought captive. If the struggle lingers, I ask Him if this is an issue I need to address by a lifestyle change. It may be the top of an iceberg exposing a deeper issue.

I also allow my emotions to be real. If I feel disappointed with God, I tell Him. I also tell Him the truth about Himself—not because He needs to hear it, but because I do. So I might say something like, "God, I am so sick and tired of people flaking out. If You really do control everything, and have all power, and I know You do, how come You don't just *make* people follow through? I know You gave us free will, but I also know You work through prayer, so right now, I'm going to ask You to cause these lazy, stubborn people to *want* to do what is right here! God, I also know I have been lazy and stubborn in my life, so give me Your grace. But also help me maintain Your standard of wanting excellence—especially since I just feel like quitting, like the rest have. Maybe deep down, God, I am jealous because it looks like other people have it easier than me. Help me work through this anger because I can't lead people if I'm mad at them and I can't lead people if I'm mad at You, so show me why I'm so mad. What am I afraid of? Why am I thinking You owe me? You don't *owe* me anything. You already gave Yourself on the cross. Seems like that should be enough for me! Why am I offtrack here?" As you follow the thought process of this prayer, you can see that the more real I was, the more yielded I became. The focus shifted from others, to God, then to what I need God to do in me.

"Real" is different for different people: It can mean crying, pacing, shouting or being so broken you can't even talk. The key is committing your thoughts honestly to a gracious God, because only then are you free to receive from Him. If I am pretending to be someone or something I am not, whom am I kidding? God can see it's an act! I have found that if I tell the truth about myself, *and* tell the truth about God, then answers come.

This Gift is Relational

Prayer is a relationship, not a time slot. I try to layer prayer into my life naturally but I also try to see that it is natural to set aside time to pray. So yes, I do pray without ceasing, like right now as I pray about how to write these words. I try to look for ways to talk to God. If I am alone in my car, I always assume that my first priority is to talk to Him. I pray as I swim, which during the winter in California is a few times a week and in the summer almost daily. I also find that walking and prayer go well together because no one can interrupt. (I don't wear my pager or cell phone in the pool or on walks.) I have mental reminders to pray: pictures on my desk, artwork on my refrigerator and notes on my mirror. I also use specific daily tasks as reminders to pray. For example, everytime I fold clothes, I pray for my family. I could choose to sit and watch TV or listen to a motivational tape at times like these but I have chosen to use some specific daily tasks as an emotional buzzer to remind me to pray and talk to God.

Each night, in bed, Bill and I pray together. I realize not all women have the freedom to pray *with* their spouse but they may have the opportunity to pray *for* their spouse. While we were guests on a television show, another guest, a song writer, told the story of how his wife prayed out loud for him each night while touching and holding him for years before he came to Christ. He was frustrated by it at first, but then he came to anticipate it and was comforted by her caring in such a profound and sincere way.

For many women, praying first thing in the morning and talking through their day with God is helpful. Since I'm not a morning person, I wait an hour or so, and pray before I start my workday, and I always pray as I work my way through my *To Do* list and agenda for the day, weighing out priorities.

I used to think that if I didn't pray a certain way (on my knees) or for a certain amount of time at a certain time of day, that I wasn't spiritual. I found that those exterior, self-imposed expectations were actually keeping me from being honest with God. I do, however, like a challenge, so I will take on new goals for this part of my relationship with God, but I refuse to believe that some people are more spiritual than others simply because they prefer different prayer styles. Comparison can be a trap that will keep you from discovering your own relationship with God.

With different ages and stages of life, our relationship with God will change and should adapt. When I was a single woman, I found that I loved to go on picnics or walks with God and spend hours journaling my thoughts to Him. As a young mother, those late night nursing moments with a child on my lap were my favorite. As my children grow, the car has become my solace and sanctuary. An airplane seat becomes a holy place as I'm strapped in for hours. God has me as His captive audience so I save big issues and decisions to pray through for those long trips. I have found it isn't the where or how or how long that is as important as the attitude of wanting to talk to God about all of life. It's the desire of anticipating time with God that helps me know my connection is strong. When the desire wanes, then I know it's time for a kick-start; a retreat, a personal getaway, a new idea or routine to wake up my quiet time.

I have already mentioned that Bill and I built our own home. My job during much of the project was to hold a level up to see if a wall or board was plumb or level—in the right place. The goal is to have the level display a bubble in the center of the instrument's markings. If it is not level or in the right place, the bubble will slide off to one side or the other. My own personal peace works the same as that bubble in the level. When my prayer life is in the right place, I usually sense an emotional peace. My personal peace is like that deep sigh that usually accompanies me as I step into a Jacuzzi. In a similar way, when I am relaxed and refreshed by God's presence in my life, I sense a deep sigh in my spirit, and an "aaahhhh" of oasis. That feeling is an indicator that I am closer to the balance God has for my life.

The Gift of Celebration

Barbara Johnson, the Erma Bombeck of the Christian community, adds humor and celebration into her life by taking a day off the first day of each month. I also take joke breaks—all day, nearly every day. A joke or funny story will take priority over almost anything. I call Bill and leave them on his email or voicemail. I drop by his office, and slide them under his door if he's in a meeting or counseling session. He interrupts my writing often with, "So have you heard the one ..." Humorous books and tapes are a part of our budget! My friends all know this, so I get funny emails from all over.[21]

"Silliness is very serious stuff," says Dr. Lee Berk, of Loma Linda University Medical Center. Patty Wooten, nurse and author of *Compassionate Laughter: Jest for Your Health* agrees. While Wooten visits patients wearing a clown outfit, Berk and his research partner, Dr. Stanley Tan, have pioneered a new field of medicine: *psychoneuronimmunology*, or the effects of laughter on the immune system.

Doctors showed funny videos to patients then noted a measurable decrease in stress hormones and an increase in natural painkillers, a rise in "T" cells which help organize the immune system's response, a rise in antibody immunoglobulin A which fights respiratory infections, more gamma interferon, a hormone that causes the immune system to turn on, and B cells that produce antibodies that fight harmful microorganisms and more Complement 3 which help the antibodies pierce infected or dysfunctional cells.[22]

This field of medicine started when Norman Cousins got relief from his degenerative disease when he laughed his way through funny videos. Even our brain benefits. Peter Derks of the College of William and Mary notes, "When we get a joke, there is a change in brain wave activity; we have solved an incongruity."[23] While laughter is no substitute for traditional medicine, it is great to have such a handy resource to harness good health.

The Gift of Hope

Laughter is good medicine. So is hope. For most of my married life, one or both of us have run our own businesses. Any entrepreneur quickly discovers it is often feast or famine. When the work is there, it is often there in piles. When we face deadlines like those, we set up "light at the end of the tunnel celebrations." Just thinking that in a week you might be lying on some sandy, sunny beach with a good novel and great company makes the work seem lighter.

When I work with women going through the trauma of an unwelcome divorce, I encourage them to do something nice for themselves each day. It can be as simple as a bubble bath or reading a women's magazine, but each day, somehow, they are to give themselves permission to have hope. Court dates are to be followed with dinner out with a safe Christian friend or her support group. Weekends without the kids are times for her to allow God to refresh her life. Conferences, reading a book at the beach, a vacation with other solid Christian friends, can all renew hope.

If you are going through a season of darkness because of a wayward child, a long-term illness, caretaking a loved one, or another strenuous life transition, place a light at the end of the tunnel. Plan something into your schedule that will allow you to receive from God.

Throw a personal party. What are some things that cost little or nothing that help you celebrate life? Make a list of these. Choose one thing off the list to do this week. As you celebrate, hope will be revitalized. For example, when I travel through Chicago O'Hare airport, I enjoy riding through an indoor canopy of light and music that extends over the moving sidewalk. I may race through other portions of the airport, but I stop and take my time and just enjoy this brief oasis of art. On less professional days, I sneak off to the children's section of a bookstore and read children's books—without my kids! (Okay, I usually buy one to take home to them, but not always!) Some days I just choose to take longer to get ready. I host my own personal spa day which includes a bubble bath by candlelight, a facial mask and lotion from Hawaii (it doesn't cost any more, but I do have to order it to have on hand!) Somedays, the celebration is simply a walk at sunset.

Receive the Gift

Dr. Hart wraps up some words of wisdom that can extend many of our lives: "To avoid cardiovascular disease and other stress-related disorders, it is not enough to eat the right foods and keep cholesterol low. This is important, but it is not enough! It is not enough to exercise regularly and even take regular vacations. To protect yourself…you must learn how to switch off your production of adrenaline when it is no longer needed, and stop using it for non-emergency life situations….It means controlling the problem at its source."[24]

Dr. Hart encourages some simple but practical methods for curbing the overuse of adrenaline: sleep 8-10 hours a night, learn to manage your negative, driving emotions, (so next time someone says "Chill out!" take them up on their offer and do it). Exercise and a daily time to unwind will help you manage your addiction to adrenaline overload. He also recommends planning recovery time into your schedule after high-adrenaline-use times.

When I travel, I do work on the plane on the trip out, but I save a new novel, great book or journaling for the way back. By setting up healthy rewards, the work seems less like work. And the reward system did start with God! "Everyone who competes in the games goes into strict training. They do it to get a crown that will not last; but we do it to get a crown that will last forever" (1 Corinthians 9:25). God will reward us for our work, but notice how the verse begins—with strict training—like an athlete. If we don't watch over our lives, no one else will. God wants you to value you. I like Paul's spin on what a "crown" is. "For what is our hope, our joy, or the crown in which we will glory in the presence of our Lord Jesus when he comes? Is it not you?" (1 Thessalonians 2:19.) Paul's hope, joy and crown were relationships, people were the payoff. *You* are someone's crown. Most likely, you are many people's crown.

When I watch how crowns are treated by homecoming queens, Rose Parade princesses, pageant winners and the monarchs, the crowns are always handled with care. Crowns receive special TLC. Can you grant yourself permission for some tender loving care today?

Putting the Pieces Together

How are you taking care of your temple? Are you balanced emotionally, physically, mentally and spiritually? What lifestyle choices do you think God would like you to make so you can receive the gift of hope again? Do you need more emotional connection, physical activity, nutrition or rest, or is it contemplation or celebration that would renew your hope? Give yourself a gift today. Choose one area to begin taking small steps in. Remember, "Small steps, taken consistently, add up in a big way over time!"

The Place
That Holds the Key

*How can I keep from
blowing my life apart?*

There is a sin, a secret sin, which someone now is keeping. She tells herself, "It's no big deal, it's personal. It hurts no one, so in my life I'm keeping."

Envy makes jealousy, jealousy makes flirting, flirting makes opportunity, opportunity makes temptation, temptation makes possibility, possibility makes intrigue, intrigue makes excitement,

excitement makes an invitation, invitation makes an affair, an affair breaks a marriage vow, a broken marriage vow breaks

> Her husband's heart
> Her children's hearts
> Her parents' hearts
> Her friends' hearts
> Her pastor's heart
> Her leader's heart
> Her Lord's heart
> Her witness
> Her future
> Her children's future
> Her finances

Her secret sin ripples.

Her children now must spend hours repairing, rebuilding, reestablishing trust in a hope that they can go against the statistic that weighs against them—that kids from broken homes tend to repeat the pattern. All of those hours they could have been learning, building and moving forward are instead used trying to recover from the emotional setback.

Her friends have to spend hours trying to convince her of the consequences of her actions, hours repairing the damage to Christ's name she brought on the community, and hours of childcare during the hours and hours of court battles and lawyer appointments. Her friends are robbed of time that could have been used moving people forward, rather than regrouping, repairing and restoring. Those who care for her children spend hours more, nurturing, caring and rebuilding each child. The ripples of divorce are felt in every classroom, every boardroom and office. Precious time is wasted because two people acted on a hidden thought.

Her pastor now has hours and hours of appointments to help those victimized by the wake of her sin—he can't use that time to share Christ or prepare a sermon or minister to the sick or dying or a variety of other evangelistic activities. Bill and I estimate that for the one sin of someone committing the act of adultery, *each* of us then must spend *approximately 100 hours of ministry time* helping all those hurt in the wake (and that's if the person repents). That includes time helping the adulterer realign his or her life. If he or she doesn't repent, and continues in the sin and continues on through with a divorce, that number quickly doubles to *over 200 hours of ministry time taken* to help all in its wake cope with the effects. And it's not just the pastor's time that is affected! *Every person who is a part of the sinning person's life and is a support to her life and family spends a similar amount of time and energy. Thousands of hours are spent trying to overcome the ramifications of one person's wrong choice.* The sexual act took only moments, but the time it takes to repair the damage is several hundred hours, which could have all been spent sharing the good news of Christ's love.

Compare the hours and hours to the instantaneous moment it takes to obey. God's Spirit speaks to your heart, "Don't do it. It's sin."

You say, "Okay, Lord. Thanks for your Holy Spirit's leading."

That's it! In just seconds, obedience is accomplished. People often ask leaders like me—and like many of you—how we can accomplish so much. I think this is the key: we obey. (And if we are surrounded by those who also obey: our husband, children, co-workers and so on our life is further simplified by obedience.) An obedient life is not encumbered by a weight of sin, so we can run the race before us that God has set *freely!*

And it is not just the sin of infidelity that causes such dramatic ripples—all sin does. This is just one example of the results, the ripples of hurt and pain sin causes. There was a sin, a secret sin, that someone once was keeping. It became a sin, a public sin, and now everyone is weeping.

The Fragrance of Obedience

Just as sin leaves a wake of destruction and devastation, so obedience leaves a ripple of hope, joy and peace. What sin takes, obedience gives.

Natalie is my associate director of women's ministry. She recommitted her life to Christ as a result of our soccer sideline talks. Natalie has grown into a woman who is very sensitive to God's call and prompting on her heart. My husband asked Natalie to contact a woman and gave her a phone number. Natalie called the woman (I'll call her Jan), and wrote down the address to her home, 843 Canyon Run. She set off for a morning meeting. She navigated her way to the door of a woman's home she had never met. Natalie knocked at the door and asked for Jan. The man who answered the door invited her in and went to get the woman. Natalie sat alone in the front room for a very long time. An uncomfortably long time.

Finally, a frail woman slowly made her way into the room. Natalie could tell she was very ill.

"Jan?" Natalie asked, puzzled because, though she had never met Jan before, this woman looked vaguely familiar.

"Oh, that's not me. I'm Lori."

Natalie whispered an "I'm sorry...I...umm...came to give some discipleship training for my church...aahh..." Natalie leaned forward as if to rise and leave. She wasn't sure whether to stay or go so she prayed.

"No, please don't go. I think God sent you."

Natalie thought, *Yeah, it is obvious why You sent me here, God. This woman is going to die.*

"I have some questions that I need to know the answers to…and I think I know you…from basketball…at the gym."

Then Natalie recognized her as a parent of children near her own children's ages. They had talked before, but Lori's health had deteriorated so quickly Natalie hadn't recognized her.

Natalie and Lori talked for a long time. When Natalie left Lori that day, Lori knew that when the cancer finally won out, she'd be in the presence of God. She had come to know and be sure of her personal relationship with God.

When Natalie got home she immediately called me. "Pam, I have to tell you what just happened."

Natalie relayed the entire story, including the fact that when she pulled into Lori's driveway she knew she was at the right house, and the address on the Post-It® note where she'd scribbled the address was the same as Lori's home—Natalie had written 843 Canyon Run. (After calling Jan to say she was running late, she discovered Jan's address was 829.) God had led Natalie to Lori that day. Natalie contacted my husband, Bill, who visited with the family and Natalie continued to visit, but in a few days Lori was gone. Bill performed the funeral and Lori's family has come to experience God's love for them.

Natalie and I have often talked about how God will move heaven and earth to get people who have a searching heart the information they need. "All I know, Pam, is that every morning I pray, *God use me.* That day with Lori, it was the weirdest experience. It was like I was watching God—and I knew what He wanted me to do.

"During the time that this happened, I look back and see that it was one of the most obedient seasons of my life. I tried to be obedient in the littlest things, and that helped me to be in tune to God's leading at a big time. There are times I go back and look at that address just to remember God's power and how He leads."

The Provision of Obedience

There are times I know beyond a shadow of a doubt that someone's actions or reactions toward me were a direct result of their obedience to God.

Years ago, when Bill and I were newlyweds and struggling to make ends meet as we pushed our way through school, a friend handed us a small black case. Kaye was also a volunteer in the youth ministry. She had just been through a really rough time in her own personal life. She was reworking her life, getting a fresh start. She handed me the black case that looked a little like a wallet. Kaye said, "This was lost for weeks. I thought I really needed what was inside, but the longer it was lost, the more I realized God wanted me to release it to Him. I told him if I found it I would do with it what He wanted. The more I prayed, the more I sensed it should go to you two. I don't know why. I just knew I had to obey and say yes to God. Yesterday I found it. Now, I am giving it to you."

With a quick hug Kaye handed me the case and turned to walk away. Inside the black plastic wallet was several hundred dollars. I knew this was a huge sacrifice for Kaye. We'd been in the same small group, praying for each other's needs all year. I also knew Kaye well enough that if she gave this out of obedience to God, she meant it. But Kaye had no idea why we needed it. She couldn't because just days before, Bill and I had decided he needed to finish school and enter full time vocational ministry. No one knew yet. We had no idea how we'd afford the educational costs. But we trusted God that if we were meant to go into Christian leadership, God would somehow make up the difference between our salaries and the enormous need ahead. Kaye's gift was the first of a patchwork quilt of gifts given to us by friends, family and church members who sacrificially obeyed God so Bill could receive a seminary education.

The Strength of Obedience

After seminary, we came back to the same home church that sent us there and served in youth ministry. One of our favorite families was moving to Atlanta. The circumstances around the move were strained. Carol, now a single mom, was leaving our youth staff to finish a degree program and find a fresh start for herself and her three teen-age kids.

They were packing up their beautiful colonial home, and I wanted to stop and say good bye and offer moral support. I had called ahead to ask if I could come by and if Carrie, her junior high daughter, would mind watching my two preschoolers for a few minutes while I chatted with Carol. Carrie said "sure" and I headed over. I walked in, gave Carol a hug and she called Carrie downstairs to which Carrie replied, "On my way, just a minute."

I held my two-year-old by the hand as we headed for the kitchen. I spotted a wonderful antique doll, ready to be carefully packed away. I exclaimed, "Oh, Carol. How beautiful! I haven't seen a doll like this since I was a very little girl. My great-grandmother had one and I remember I used to love to touch her, hold her, look at her. They just don't make dolls this beautiful anymore."

"Oh, thank you. Yes, you can hardly find china dolls like that anymore. This one is special. Even her arms and legs are china and her eyes open and close. It must have been very expensive. At least that's what I was told by my friend who gave it to me. She was a very kind, elderly neighbor that I used to help with some things she needed done around her home, and when she packed up her things to move in with her family because of her failing health, she wanted me to have it." Carol had been talking to me from the kitchen where she was making tea. I was standing in the dining room, the beautiful, delicate China doll in one hand, and my sweet little boy's hand in my other. I gently set the doll back where I had found it.

I walked a few steps forward and I heard a loud crash. I looked over. My son had reached up to grab the fragile china doll and he held it by one leg. Because he was so short, the doll's head had smashed as it hit Carol's hardwood floor.

I know I cried. Carol cried. That made my son cry. And Carol just wrapped her arms around me and my little boy and we all stood in the dining room crying for a moment. I know I said "I'm sorry" hundreds of times. I felt horrible. I had come to give comfort and here Carol was comforting me. So many of her treasured hopes and dreams had recently come crashing down at her feet and now I had caused one more broken treasure. I knew I couldn't offer to replace it. The doll was irreplaceable. And even if I could find one somewhere in some antique store, I could never have afforded it. We were barely making ends meet as it was. Carol said something just as remarkable as the things she always said, "I have come to see that things, even beautiful precious things are still just things, Pam. Relationships are my most valued treasures. Now, come, sit and let's have some tea." It's been over 13 years since that day and I still remember it like yesterday.

Obedience is like that. It leaves a fragrance of life, health and hope wherever it is found. Obedience is so sweet, and its effects so world changing. How can we cultivate it in our lives?

A Heart-to-Heart Connection

Jesus pulls His disciples together toward the end of His life and in John chapters 14–17 He relays the most vital information they will need to know as the mantle of ministry passes to them. Over and over Christ emphasizes obedience. He does it in a variety of ways, but the message is all the same. He explains, "He who has My commandments and keeps them, he it is who loves

Me; and he who loves Me shall be loved by My Father and I will love him and will disclose myself to him" (John 14:21 NASB). The secret to being a woman God can use is plainly stated. The answer to how to know God's will is listed. *Obey.*

Jesus goes on to try to answer the deeper question of our heart, "But how do we know what to obey?"

"If anyone loves Me, he will keep My word; and My Father will love him and We will come to him, and make Our abode with him" (John 14:23 NASB). When we ask, "What is Your will, God?" we are looking for a concrete list of do's and don'ts. We want a typed out *To Do* list. We want the meeting's agenda. But God wants a connection with us. That's the word picture He begins to paint throughout the next few chapters.

You Are the Branches

In John 15:1–17 Jesus gives us a picture of our relationship with Him. "I am the vine, you are the branches" (John 15:5). This is a picture of the grape orchards so common in the hills and valleys of Israel. Jesus is the vine. All the nutrients come from Him. His roots sink into the ground to gather all we need, and then He channels it all to us. All we do is receive it and blossom! We aren't just any kind of branch—we're a pruned branch, ready to grow. Jesus explains that He did the pruning: "You are already clean because of the word I have spoken to you" (John 15:3). *You are clean*: ready to grow, prepared for fruit bearing.

As clean branches, we cannot decide to just take off and do our own thing. We'd die. A branch must be connected to the vine to produce fruit. That's why Jesus finishes verse 5, "…he who abides in Me and I in Him, he bears much fruit; for apart from Me you can do nothing."

No abiding, no fruit. It is like a math formula: A+B=C. Jesus in me + me abiding in Him = fruit. So what does abiding mean and how do we do it? In this case, the meaning is to *stay*, continue, dwell, endure, be present, remain, stand, tarry—in other words, don't go anywhere![1] It's like we're pitching a tent and we've taken up residence in Him.

The results of abiding are given in verse 11, "These things I have spoken to you, that My joy may be in you, and that your joy may be made full" (NASB). And isn't joy one of the things we women are really after? We love the feeling of being on top of the world, at peace with ourselves and those around us. We love the excitement and adventure of seeing a plan come together. We love the rush, the jazz, the thrill of deep emotional connectedness. Wrap up all those emotions and a few other positive feelings and that's how we picture joy. Jesus is saying that joy, and the deep, "everything will work out no matter what" peace is His joy, and it only comes to us when we abide. There is no other way to have the sense that the pieces are falling together. It only comes when we abide, stay, remain or *camp out* in Him!

You Are Friends

Jesus moves to a new picture, a more intimate one. In verse 15 He says, "No longer do I call you slaves, for the slave does not know what his master is doing; but I have called you friends, for all things that I have heard from My Father I have made known to you" (NASB). Jesus has the right to call us slaves or servants, after all we were bought with a price—His blood. But He wants us to be more than people who "owe Him." He knows how our minds work.

Have you ever owed someone money? Every time you see them you feel guilty. You know that they know you owe them. They may not act any differently toward you than before, but you know there is something there and neither of you has to say anything. If you go on owing, you may even want to avoid seeing that person altogether because you feel so bad about not repaying. Jesus doesn't want a strained relationship built on a foundation of guilt, He wants to be our friend, even though we still owe Him, and always will! He knows there is no amount of money, there is no amount of good works, there is nothing we can do that will repay what He did for us on Calvary, so He changes the relationship entirely. He calls us friends.

Take a minute and describe your relationship with one of your best friends. How does it function?

My best friend wants what is best for me. She is willing to be inconvenienced to see that I have what I need to succeed in all of my life, home, work, ministry and relationships. She and I talk regularly and when we talk it is on a deeper level. She can tell from my voice over the phone when I'm stressed or discouraged. She can tell from my body language if I am feeling great or anxious.

If I describe my friendship with my husband, I would also add in that he wants to know all about me and I want to know all about him. We would also go to the ends of the earth to help each other out. I know he would die for me, I know he would set aside his wants, needs and desires if I needed him to. When we are separated by ministry or business, we can feel the strain of being apart. I once told him, "Honey, I'm just no good without you." I feel that when we are together we are so much stronger, we think clearer and we make a winning team.

Friendship with Jesus is *all* that and so much more. He knows our every thought. He knows our every need even before we do. He sees our lives in totality and how they relate to the framework of history and He can work all things for our good. He created time so He can see from beginning to end what is best for us, and He has all the power to carry out all the plans He has for us. He placed His Holy Spirit in us and He describes the work the Holy Spirit can produce in our lives if we are yielded: "Love, joy, peace, patience, kindness, goodness, faithfulness, gentleness and self-control." In John 16, He says the Holy Spirit convicts concerning sin, righteousness and judgment, and He will lead us into all truth and He will glorify God.

If I am a friend of God, I will want to know all about Him. As I know about Him, then I will know what He wants me to do.

The Big Picture

There are certain methods that have helped me know God's will. I like to parallel them to the same way we learn to interpret scripture. If I am lost in a city, I pick up a map. If I don't have one, I go to the highest point I can find so I can get my bearings by looking at the big picture. The same thing is true of discerning God's will. Women who have taken the time, energy and work to study the Bible cover to cover, are more confident in their own ability to hear God's voice. Having an overall general understanding of God's book helps us understand God and understand how He works. By layering the big picture into your life on a regular basis, your framework for hearing the voice of God stays in place.

Try one of these ideas to layer the big picture into your life:

1. Read the Bible Through in a Year. There are many great programs to help you do this. Your own Bible might even have a plan for accomplishing this in a year. The *One Year Bible* is also a resource you might consider. My favorite way to read the Bible through is a quiet time resource called *Walk Thru the Bible.*[2] It is a magazine that comes monthly to your home and it daily leads you devotionally through the Bible. It has information on history, charts, diagrams and practical inspirational thoughts to feed you emotionally, spiritually and intellectually. *Walk Thru* also offers weekend seminars to walk a person through the main events of the Bible in a memorable way.

2. Study the Bible Chronologically. I have a poster in my office that explains how the Bible came from its original papyrus form to the Bible in my own language that sits on my desk today. Seeing the Bible and how God has sustained His Word gives me confidence that He will sustain me. I also like the *Wall Chart of World History* and the *Christian History Chart of Events in Church History*. As I see how God has had a plan for men and women throughout history, I am reassured that He has a plan for me. I also enjoy the *Chronological Bible*, which is compiled in the order the books were written rather than the traditional Genesis–Revelation format we are used to. By seeing the chronology, I get the point driven home devotionally that God is a God of order. He lays foundations, then builds on them. He called Israel and gave her a mission to exhibit His character to all who came in contact with her. He established the family. He called Abraham, then Moses to lead a nation, a chosen one. He set down a law so it would be a tutor of right and wrong. The law showed people that on their own, they couldn't meet the standard. When they needed a Savior, He sent a Savior. The Savior lived among men first, then asked for a response, "Who do you say that I am?" (Matthew 16:15).

By seeing the big picture, I gain a philosophy of life that is the backdrop to my daily decisions. For example, since God first laid down the law and *then* held men accountable for it, as a parent I should also instruct before I discipline. How can people obey when they didn't know there was a rule to obey? Because God is a God of order, and He has moved patiently throughout history, if I am rushing around forcing a decision, and everything seems unsure, unclear and confusing, then chances are it isn't His will. Because I see over and over again that God came to individual people with a calling, even when He was giving instructions for entire nations, I should assume that God today will call individuals, then build a ministry around them. That God blesses people and not programs is a methodology I picked up from seeing the big picture.

I might feel overwhelmed if I think I have to single-handedly turn the morality of a nation back to God, but if I go back to the big picture, I will see that God worked with leaders, squared away their integrity, and then there was a trickledown effect that took place among the people. I can watch over my own integrity and I don't have to think I am a watchdog for the world's. The impossible just became possible because I stepped back and took a look at the big picture.

3. Get to Know the Character of God. Study the major themes. By doing theme studies of the Bible, as in what does the Bible say about money, sex, power, children and mothering, I gain an overall picture of God's heart on any given subject. It helps me get to know the character of God better. Study His names. The names of God, the Father, the Son and the Holy Spirit will all reveal who God is in a rich way. By studying who God is, I get to see how He thinks, acts and relates to people. When I am in a tough spot, especially when I have to make a quick decision, I go back and ask: "What would God's character have me do?" I think that is one reason behind the popularity of the WWJD? bracelets that have sold in the millions. It is a simple question—but it does assume *you know* what God would do! That means you have to have a backlog of good information from daily quiet times logged away so you have something that the Holy Spirit can draw on!

4. Context. A key point in learning to exposit (or dissect to gain meaning) the Scripture, is to look at a verse within its context. What verses are around it, what chapter comes before and after and what are those chapters talking about? What book is it in? Who wrote that book, to whom and why? As I look at the context, I gain clarity on what a verse means. I gain a more accurate interpretation.

I have found the same thing to be true in decision making. When people hire employees they do background checks and references. That is one way of looking at a person in his or her context. Before I allowed my children to go to a person's home, I accompanied them. By seeing someone's surroundings you learn a lot about them, their value and priorities.

Focusing the Picture

After looking at the big picture, when you study the Bible you next start to narrow your field of scope. You can make outlines, diagram sentences and do word studies. When making a decision (especially an important one—like whom to date, marry, how to raise children, vocation—things that have long-term ramifications on my life), I like to have as much information as possible in front of me. It is not uncommon for me to say, "I will have to get back to you on that. I need more information to make an informed decision." I make charts, pro and con lists and graphs if I think it will help me see the issue in a clearer light.

When you layer God's Word into your life on a daily basis, you gain the ability to see things closer to the way God does. Jesus explains it as *you are in me and I am in you* (John 14:20; John 17:21). God tells us, "You have the mind of Christ" (1 Corinthians 2:16). The context for that verse explains the need for solid food from the Word, not just milk.

The Word of God is the key ingredient in protecting your heart. The Proverbs explain the priority of cardiovascular workout for our spiritual heart: "Above all else, guard your heart, for it is the wellspring of life" (Proverbs 4:23). My son Zach is a skateboarder. He does all kinds of wildly fun tricks, but he also wears protective gear and a helmet. God has protective gear for us to wear too. When we wear the gear, life is just safer!

Check out the pieces of this armor in Ephesians 6:13-17:

Therefore put on the full armor of God, so that when the day of evil comes, you may be able to stand your ground, and after you have done everything, to stand. Stand firm then, with the belt of truth buckled around your waist, with the breastplate of righteousness in place, and with your feet fitted with the readiness that comes from the gospel of peace. In addition to all this, take up the shield of faith, with which you can extinguish all the flaming arrows of the evil one. Take the helmet of salvation and the sword of the Spirit, which is the word of God.

The belt of truth: So what is truth and where do you find it? Over and over Christ says in the Gospels, "I tell you the truth..." Jesus is the truth, and John explains that Jesus is also: "The Word became flesh and made his dwelling among us. We have seen his glory, the glory of the One and Only, who came from the Father, full of grace and truth" (John 1:14). The incarnate Word is truth and the written Word He gave is truth: "Sanctify them by the truth; your word is truth" (John 17:17). The Word sets you free: "Then you will know the truth, and the truth will set you free" (John 8:32). When making decisions ask: "What is the truth in this situation?" Then pull out a concordance or use a Bible computer program to find the truth out about the issue.

The breastplate of righteousness: What is righteousness and how is it obtained? "For in the gospel a righteousness from God is revealed, a righteousness that is by faith from first to last, just as it is written: 'The righteous will live by faith'" (Romans 1:17). So righteousness comes from the gospel, and *the gospel of peace* is: "Remember Jesus Christ, raised from the dead, descended from David. This is my gospel..." (2 Timothy 2:8). We are back to Jesus, the Word! When you are facing a decision, ask: "Will this decision treat everyone rightly? Will this decision bring glory or harm to the gospel?"

The shield of faith: Romans 10:17 says, "Consequently, faith comes from hearing the message, and the message is heard through the word of Christ." The Word! *Go back to people who know the Word, ask them their opinion.* Find people who will speak the word of truth into your life. Those words will shield you from making erratic decisions.

The helmet of salvation: Is the helmet of salvation any different? "Salvation is found in no one else, for there is no other name under heaven given to men by which we must be saved." Acts 4:12 is speaking of Jesus, the living Word. How does salvation take place?

> That if you confess with your mouth, "Jesus is Lord," and believe in your heart that God raised him from the dead, you will be saved. For it is with your heart that you believe and are justified, and it is with your mouth that you confess and are saved. As the Scripture says, "Anyone who trusts in him will never be put to shame" (Romans 10:9-11).

The written Word tells the story of the living Word and we believe. The power is in the Word. If you are confused, ask yourself: "Am I listening to outside sources here? Am I placing more weight on the Word and people who know the Word—or am I trusting in the opinions of people without saving faith?"

The sword of the Spirit: Hebrews 4:12 reminds us that, "For the word of God is living and active. Sharper than any double-edged sword, it penetrates even to dividing soul and spirit, joints and marrow; it judges the thoughts and attitudes of the heart." The sharpest sword is the Word. This is the hardest question of all: "Am I taking the easy way out just because the Word is making me uncomfortable?"

I'm sure you've got the picture. The power to obey is fueled by the Word of God. The more of God's Word we take in, the more likely we will live it out.

But all of these things are just busywork if I don't have the right heart attitude. If I am simply going through the spiritual motions and in the end I know I'm just going to do what I please then I should be prepared for negative repercussions and fallout in life. I will be more likely to be a woman God can use if I simply yield my will to God's. By asking, "What do you think, God?" I am spiritually counting to ten, and that momentary pause gives God the opportunity to lead me.

In Romans all we are asked to do is yield. Yield means to voluntarily offer up something of value and put it under the control of another. Romans 6:13 clearly reveals the options and the results. "Do not offer the parts of your body to sin, as instruments of wickedness, but rather offer yourselves to God, as those who have been brought from death to life; and offer the parts of your body to him as instruments of righteousness."

It is now another math formula. If $A+B=C$ and $A+D=C$ then B and D must be the same. Abiding and yielding have the same impact—they make us *friends* of Christ.

Often, people ask me how I have accomplished so much in such a short amount of time. From the outside, people can see the nine books that have been written in five years. They see the travel schedule, and then they picture all the daily responsibilities that come with a home, children and marriage. And when they read that I am a pastor's wife and I do radio ministry they shake their heads in disbelief. They can't picture it. My schedule is just more visible. I think if many of us actually took the time to write down what we had accomplished—or need to—we'd all easily feel overwhelmed.

I could tell you to squeeze more time out of your day. I do, you do, we all do. We multi-task, we buy fancy organizers and calendars, we file, we pile, we own phone message pads that record in triplicate. We buy personal organizers, and computer software that keeps us on track, and some of us pay people to organize our life or have personal assistants—and all these things work to help you find more time in your day—but what they don't do is tell you *how* to spend that time. Only God does that. Obedience is the key.

All I know is that when I abide in Christ, when I yield to His leading and try to do *what He wants me to when He wants me to* it all works. It is like putting your hand in a glove. I am the glove, when I place myself on His hand, I move where He moves. A glove cannot move independently. Somehow, as long as I stay a glove and not try to be the hand, it all works. Moment by moment, it works.

Obedience keeps our thoughts on track, and our thoughts keep our actions on track. Laurie McIntyre, Director of Women at Elmbrook church says, "Thoughts are the forerunners to all of your actions."[3] By taking our thoughts captive as instructed in 2 Corinthians 10:5, we gain the ability to follow Jesus' lead. The word picture for taking thoughts captive is the picture of handcuffing them and throwing them into prison.[4] It is us deciding to arrest a thought. I usually say, "Don't go there!" and "What is the truth here?" Then I stand on the truth—that's why knowing the truth is so important. Truth is the prison guard of the mind. That's why the truth sets you free. Truth puts false thinking in prison instead of your thinking!

When you have a pattern of not taking thoughts captive, your rational thinking patterns begin to erode. You can no longer think clearly. For example, these stories relay accounts of how people begin to think when they don't stay on truth and take their thoughts captive:

A woman wrote to newspaper columnist Abigail Van Buren:

> Dear Abby,
>
> I am a twenty-three-year-old liberated woman who has been on the pill for two years. It's getting expensive and

I think my boyfriend should share half the cost, but I don't know him well enough to discuss money with him.

Knows him well enough for sex but not finances... hummmm...

There's an adage that crooks are so stupid they end up getting caught. What do you think?

In New York, as a female shopper exited a convenience store, a man grabbed her purse and ran. The clerk called 911 immediately and the woman was able to give them a detailed description of the snatcher. Within minutes, the police had apprehended the snatcher. They put him in the cruiser and drove back to the store. The thief was then taken out of the car and told to stand there for a positive ID. To which he replied "Yes, Officer...that's her. That's the lady I stole the purse from."

A man in South Carolina, walked into a local police station, dropped a bag of cocaine on the counter, informed the desk sergeant that it was substandard cut, and asked that the person who sold it to him be arrested immediately.

In Indiana, a man walked up to a cashier at a grocery store and demanded all the money in the register. When the cashier handed him the loot, he fled—leaving his wallet on the counter.

A man decided to rob a bank. He handed a note to the teller and told her to fill up a bag with the money. After receiving the loot, he decided that the bag was too bulky to carry out of the bank without attracting attention. So, he filled out a deposit slip, and had the teller deposit the money into his bank account.

I'd say these folks have gone way too long with out the guidance that comes from the truth! Discretion and clear thinking goes right out the window when the Word isn't in your life. Honesty becomes a hit and miss activity.

A man in our church designs computer software for the criminal justice system. One police officer relayed a story to our friend about a man he'd arrested and pulled into the lineup. Seems the crook who stole a woman's purse had said to the woman, "Give me that purse." The woman looking at the lineup was unsure of the culprit, so she asked the officer if each of the men could say, "Give me your purse." The first man in the lineup said, "I want your purse, give it to me!" and another man in the line up stepped forward and said, "That's not what I said. I said, 'Hey lady, give me that purse!'"

The same man was told that a criminal standing trial was seated in the courtroom next to his lawyer and when the lawyer for the prosecution asked a witness if she saw the perpetrator of the crime in the room, the defendant raised his hand!

Bill and I have had some equally amazing things said to us:

A woman, after smashing her husband's Rolex watch, said: "I don't understand why he is so hateful towards me."

A man who had slept with his girlfriend told us, "It must have been God's will that brought us together because the sex was so good. It felt so right."

"She looked at me funny, so I'm not going back to church." (Honest, it was really said!)

From a woman who'd had an affair with her best friend's husband and finally married him: "I just know it was God's will that I marry him because on the night of our wedding, there was a rainbow around the moon."

A new friend and I sat on the soccer sidelines as our boys played. She found out that my husband was a pastor so she began to be interested in talking to me about spiritual issues. One day she brought up palm reading. I asked her why she had her palm read. She said she wanted help in knowing what to do in her future. I explained to her that God would love to do that for her. She said, "Oh, He did, when I got my palm read."

I explained that God never tells us to do things that are opposite to what He says in his Word and his Word says that fortune tellers, tarot cards and things like that are considered divination and we are to have nothing to do with them. (Deuteronomy18:10-14)

"But it has to be okay with God. The palm reader prayed before she read my palm."

"But God is not schizophrenic. If He says don't do it, He means don't do it. It doesn't matter if the person uses Christian words or actions, it is not Christian. It isn't that we pray, it's *whom we pray to* that matters."

Stinkin' thinkin' sets in where there is no truth. The more we refuse to take our thoughts captive, the worse the thinking becomes. It's as though a callous develops over our heart and we are no longer sensitive to God's leading. Where there is a lack of truth, a sickness of thinking creeps in. On the other hand, where there is truth, there is also clarity and long-term positive fruit.

It Pays

The first Christian books I ever read were poetry-prose written by Ann Kiemel. In one of her stories, she shared that her mother always told her, "It pays, it pays to follow Jesus." That phrase, "It pays," stuck in the back of my head as a freshman college student. Whenever I came to a place where it was emotionally challenging to follow Jesus, "It pays!" would echo in my heart and mind, and I'd gain the courage to obey.

It is easier to obey when I stand on the truth that God loves me and He has my best in mind at all times. God says if He is "for us, who can be against us? He who did not spare his own Son, but gave him up for us all—how will he not also, along with him, graciously give us all things?" (Romans 8:31-32). David prayed in Psalm 17:8, knowing God would answer, "Keep me as the apple of your eye; hide me in the shadow of your wings." Jeremiah 31:3 promises, "The Lord appeared to us in the past, saying: 'I have loved you with an everlasting love; I have drawn you with loving-kindness.'" And in Psalm 32:8 we are assured: "I will instruct you and teach you in the way you should go; I will counsel you and watch over you." Believing that God loves me draws me into obedience.

When I was dating Bill, I came to a crossroad in my relationship with him and with God. I had made a list of the kind of person I wanted to someday marry by listing traits I saw in the New Testament in Christ and His disciples. It was a list of internal character qualities: loving, respectful of women, a good listener, kind and compassionate. Bill fit the list. Our hearts and plans were running in the same direction but because we were allowing God to rework our dating patterns we were both in new territory emotionally. One week in my quiet times, I became impressed with the fact that on the following weekend when I saw Bill, I would need to know where I stood on areas of physical boundaries. I knew my past pattern of letting the guy take the lead wasn't very wise so I let God take the lead this time. I studied and saw the verses that backed up my decision to remain a virgin. But I also saw a pattern, and as I prayed I became convinced that our physical relationship needed to progress forward only after tangible measures of commitment. When God said, "I love you" He demonstrated it! I thought that was a good principle!

That weekend Bill and I sat on a rock in the sunshine and talked for hours as we watched the ocean. It was one of the best days of my life. I felt so cherished, so loved, so wanted. Bill had a list of questions he wanted to ask me about and they mostly concerned our physical boundaries. How far did we think God wanted us to go and when? We navigated our conversation through, holding hands, hugging, walking arm in arm and we'd already decided God was clear about no sex before marriage—it was all the stuff in between we were concerned and confused about now. I saw on the list "kissing" and I knew God had prepared me for that weekend.

But Bill stopped short and didn't ask me about it. He took me to my friends' apartment where I was staying to get ready for our evening date. And that evening was magical too. A quiet romantic fondue dinner and a walk through the downtown district over bridges and creeks and under gas lamps on a foggy night. We walked and talked, and talked and walked and I was getting cold so Bill wrapped his arms around me and tucked me into his car to take me back to my friends. He stopped at his place first and I went in with him and it was there he asked, "Pam, can I kiss you?"

My body wanted to rush into his arms and let him kiss me over and over again but the Holy Spirit inside me reminded me of my quiet time conversations with God that I had journaled all week.

"Bill, I want to say yes, but I can't. You see I've wrecked all my past relationships because I haven't watched over this area of my life very well. I value my relationship with you too much to say yes. So until you're ready to commit to me as the person you'd like to marry, then I have to say no. If you'd like to kiss me on the cheek that would be okay...so...no. I care for you but I care for God more...so...." I trailed off as he stared at me in silence. He brushed my tear-stained cheek with fingertips for a brief moment, took my hand and drove me home in utter silence for 20 minutes.

I told him again at the door what a wonderful day I had with him and how much I loved being with him and he mumbled something about picking me up for breakfast at 8 A.M.

I opened the door and burst into tears. My girlfriends rushed toward me. "What's wrong? What's wrong?"

I told them the story and said, "Oh, I am so afraid I might have said goodbye to the best man I've ever had in my life. I just knew God had been preparing me and I had a choice, Bill's will or God's will in my life. I had to choose God."

One of my friends tried to comfort me, "Pam, we all know Bill and he wants God's best in his life and in yours. You have to trust his character. If he really is the godly man he appears to be, he'll handle this."

Another said, "You have to trust God. After all, He got you into this thing!"

So the group of us prayed together. They slept and I lay awake a while longer, wondering what morning's light would bring.

Bill was smiling when he picked me up in the morning. He drove me to a beautiful scenic precipice where we could see the bright morning sun dance across the ocean waves. "Pam, I didn't say anything last night because I didn't know what to say. I've never been in the presence of a woman as committed to God as you are. Just being with you strengthens my walk with God. Pam, I was hurt and embarrassed last night. I felt like I should have been the one who protected our purity, that's why I was quiet. But I want you to know I totally agree with you. You are the best thing that has ever happened to me and I don't want our relationship to crumble because we didn't watch over our sexuality. I won't play games with your heart. When I am ready to marry you, then I will ask to kiss you."

A few months later, at the same beach house where Bill first asked me for a kiss, he bent on his knee, sang a song he wrote especially for me, then asked me to marry him. I of course said, "Yes!" Then he asked, "May I kiss you?"

"Yes!!!" And it was a kiss worth waiting for. Bill and I often reflect back on that decision to obey God in the very difficult place of our sexuality. We have come to see that our choice to wait forced us to find other ways to communicate our feelings and our love. Because of this our romantic relationship was strengthened and our sexual relationship has always been very rich and exciting and fulfilling—even 20 years later! We think it is because God taught us to communicate so we can communicate about anything—even the most intimate details of a sexually intimate relationship.

Our decision landed in a grey area, one not specifically detailed in scripture. There is no Relationships 1:7 that details what and when to do things in a dating relationship, but there are verses that encourage a pure heart and a pure mind. Because of our knowledge of the Bible and because our hearts were attuned to God's leading in our lives, when God spoke to my heart, it was not ambiguous. We heard loud and clear what the Holy Spirit wanted us to do—we only had to choose to obey.

I truly believe we would not have the strong marriage, or a marriage ministry with several books, a radio program and T.V. opportunities, had I made a different choice. God clearly laid out what He wanted me to do. All I had to do was trust He had my best interests in mind. Obedience is trust in the *person* of God. Obedience pays.

❊ ❊ ❊

Putting the Pieces Together

Is there a decision you are needing clarity on? Try one of the big picture methods and see if you can gain God's perspective on the issue? Is there an issue that is causing you to have a difficult time obeying God? As you look back over your life, do you see any pivotal decisions when obedience made the difference? Are there pivotal moments you'd wished you'd obeyed? Try to list five or six times you know obedience made the difference in the course your life took. Remember, God does have your best interests in mind! Find a verse that speaks of God's care to your heart and memorize it. Are you feeling emotionally distraught over a circumstance? Ask yourself: "What is the truth about this situation? What is my part? What is God's part?" Ruth Graham, wife of evangelist Billy Graham, says, "You do the possible and trust God with the impossible."[5] God cares more about you finding and walking in His will than even you do! He will lead you. My favorite verse that shows God's caring guidance is Isaiah 31:21, "Whether you turn to the right or to the left, your ears will hear a voice behind you, saying, 'This is the way; walk in it.'" The key is to have ears to hear the whisper of the Holy Spirit and a heart that will follow.

10

Places of the Heart

What matters most?

$\mathcal{I}$was looking forward to this trip to Oklahoma. My father had been raised in the state and coming to speak here felt a little like coming home. After I landed, two leaders met me in the airport. I immediately knew this trip was going to be different from many of the others. They had an excitement that was contagious. I sensed God's favor was with this group as we chatted over lunch. No one ate much lunch because the more we talked the less important the food became. After lunch, they asked me if I wanted to stop at a local historical monument and I answered in the affirmative.

The monument was the site of the April 19, 1995 bombing of the federal building in Oklahoma City. A chain link fence guarded the site of the now-leveled building that is being turned into a park. The fence was covered for blocks and blocks with memorabilia. (I learned later that there were warehouses full of gifts from the outpouring of the public's hearts.) As I walked that fence, I knew I would never again be the same woman. On the fence were spontaneous gifts of people who had come to the site. Hundreds and hundreds of teens must have taken off their WWJD?[1] bracelets. There were T-shirts from clubs, youth groups and churches with signatures and verses written on them. There were Christmas and birthday presents meant for the victims who had died in the bombing. Wreaths with eulogies and poems and pictures of the victims decorated the somber fence like Christmas lights wrapped around a mile-long gravestone. Bibles opened to a specific comforting verse were affixed as beacons of hope. Hymnals with song pages like "It is Well with my Soul" dotted the fence line. At one end of the memorial stands a towering white sculpture of Jesus, head bowed and the plaque at His feet simply reads "Jesus wept" (John 11:35).

That weekend, as I talked, wept, read and prayed with those dear women of Edmond, Oklahoma, I realized they had one advantage over most of the rest of the world. They had ordered priorities. Coming face to face with the brevity of life had forever changed them too. They knew what was significant because they had each stared down death face to face. Because one action caused the loss of 168 people, not many in the state went untouched by grief.

It's Life and Death

It was a normal workday, 9:02 in the morning. Coffee cups were in hand or on the desks of the workers of the building. A majority of the workers in the building were women, many single mothers, trying their best to provide for their families. Some of them took advantage of the day care center on the building's lower level.

At 9:02 A.M. a bomb exploded and lives stopped. All the survivors, those inside and those outside, had to make a choice about what was really important, what was indeed significant, and then they proceeded ahead. For most it was a split second instantaneous decision. Years of moral lessons heard in church, at home and in the community ran to the forefront of their minds. People, people matter most.

Soon signs sprung up around the city, declaring a source of hope and encouragement. One read, *God is our refuge and strength* (Psalm 46:1) and another simply read, *Good will overcome evil.*

Children of the Light

How can good overcome evil? The idea of being light and the idea of being God's temple are connected. Just as the temple in Jerusalem was the symbol of God's holiness, righteousness and truth, so we too, as the church, are the representation of God's righteousness on earth. Paul expresses this idea when he says, "For you were once darkness, but now you are light in the Lord. Live as children of light" (Ephesians 5:8).

Just as light emanated from the temple and proclaimed the glory of God, God's life emanates from us and proclaims the transforming power of God. In so doing, our lives expose the darkness of unrighteous living.

> Living together as a body, we build one another up and grow toward maturity. As family, we find our attitudes and

> values changed as love becomes the touchstone of our
> lives. As God's temple we find our lives taking on a holi-
> ness which exposes evil for what it is. Living together as
> a holy temple means rejecting dark things and building
> our commitment to goodness, righteousness, and truth.[2]

How does the church expose evil? By mounting a crusade, or
picketing? Hardly. Evil is exposed by providing an example of
righteousness.

> Paul put it this way: "Everything exposed by the light
> becomes visible, for it is light that makes everything vis-
> ible" (Ephesians 5:13-14). As children of light, we reveal
> darkness for what it is. In the light shed by the holiness
> of God's people, evil is revealed as evil.[3]

So what did the temple look like when God's glory took residence? First Kings 8:10-11 explains what it looked like when the
glory of the Lord took residence in the temple Solomon built:
"When the priests withdrew from the Holy Place, the cloud filled
the temple of the Lord. And the priests could not perform their
service because of the cloud, for the glory of the Lord filled his
temple." Second Chronicles 7:1-3 adds to the picture and says,
"Fire came down from heaven and consumed the burnt offering
and the sacrifices, and the glory of the Lord filled the
temple...When all the Israelites saw the fire coming down and
the glory of the Lord above the temple, they knelt on the pavement with their faces to the ground, and they worshiped and gave
thanks to the Lord, saying, 'He is good; his love endures forever.'"

The prophet Ezekiel tries to explain what the glory of the Lord
looked like to him, "Like the appearance of a rainbow in the
clouds on a rainy day, so was the radiance around him. This was
the appearance of the likeness of the glory of the LORD. When I
saw it, I fell facedown, and I heard the voice of one speaking"
(Ezekiel 1:28). He notes later, "Then the glory of the LORD rose

from above the cherubim and moved to the threshold of the temple. The cloud filled the temple, and the court was full of the radiance of the glory of the LORD" (Ezekiel 10:4). That is the picture God is trying to explain when He says we are children of the light. His glory, revealed through our lives, will have a dramatic impact on people.

You are children of the light, seems to not say what we should do or be, but rather *who we are* because we dwell in His presence. His presence has a natural affect on us—and on the world around us.

There are times when we can ponder, plan and think out our actions and reactions, but this title of *children of the light* seems to lead us to the conclusion that when we are in Christ we *are* different. We have radically different reactions, even when there is no time to think, no time to wonder, no time to rationalize and no time to write a flowchart or business plan. The context is that Ephesians 5:8 is followed by verses 15 and 16: "Therefore be careful how you walk, not as unwise men, but as wise, making the most of your time, because the days are evil."

God adds to the picture when He says, "You are all sons of the light and sons of the day. We do not belong to the night or to the darkness. So then, let us not be like others, who are asleep, but let us be alert and self-controlled" (1 Thessalonians 5:5-6). *You are sons of the light, sons of the day.* You and I are to be alert, in control of our senses.

What's Your Reaction Time?

Driving tests often test a person's reaction time to see if he or she is able to avoid obstacles and stop in time to avoid calamity. The doctor tests your reaction when he taps your knee to see if your reflexes are working. As children of the light, our natural reflex is to walk in the light. Those not in fellowship with God are drawn to darkness. Those connected to Christ are drawn toward a life that emanates light.

Heather Taylor, a college student studying emergency medicine, was one of the first to arrive on the bomb scene with Dr. Carl Spangler that April day in Oklahoma. Heather, having not slept a wink in the previous 24 hours, said:

> Dr. Spangler decided we needed to set up the triage (an area where victims are given priority according to their condition), as no one else was doing it. More and more people started to arrive with the equipment we needed. This was the moment when I got scared. Dr. Spangler gave me triage tags and told me to follow him around and tag the people minor, moderate, critical or dead. You would think that you wouldn't waste your time on the dead, but tagging the dead kept people from going back to them trying to save them....Our first priority was to establish a triage team. Dr. Spangler got on the intercom of the fire truck and told everyone to listen. I was amazed at how he took charge of the situation and everyone listened to him. He told everyone that he wanted twenty paramedics, twenty physicians, and twenty ICU nurses. He looked at me and told me that I was to stay with him wherever he went. I just nodded.[4]

Heather just nodded. Obeyed. Served. Heather obeyed the doctor without question. She had a desire to obey out of a sense of trust. When we walk in the light, our heart wants to obey. We have an intrinsic yearning to serve. The higher the stakes, the more likely we are to want to obey and serve. We trust God, so we serve God. I think it is because when we come to know God personally our role is changed from that of a citizen of society to an ambassador. Just as ambassadors seek to reconcile countries, we seek to reconcile people to God. Because we have a heart for reconciliation, our priorities shift. We can see what is imperative.

"We are therefore Christ's ambassadors, as though God were making his appeal through us. We implore you on Christ's behalf: Be reconciled to God" (2 Corinthians 5:20). The imperative is made clear because God's appeal is going out through *us*. *You are an ambassador!* God is offering reconciliation to Himself. When we look at people, we should have the same heart as the people at the site of the Oklahoma City bombing, or the same thoughts as the captains and crew on the sinking *Titanic*: How many can be rescued? As many as we possibly can. Who is in eminent peril? We need to get to them first. This is the heartbeat of an ambassador for Christ.

Ambassadors who serve in foreign countries realize they will never totally feel comfortable in the host country because it is not their homeland. The same is true of us. If we truly have the heart of an ambassador, we will realize that our citizenship is in heaven (Philippians 3:20).

Ambassadors also seek to learn the language and the culture of their host country so they can be more effective. Ambassadors want what is best for the people of their host country. What is physically best, emotionally best and socially and politically best but primarily what is spiritually best. Proverbs 13:17 explains the result of a heart that wants the best for the host people: "Faithful ambassadors bring health" (NKJV).

On August 6, 1945, 15-year-old Yoshikosan Taguchi sat in a classroom in a Christian school in Japan. She deeply resented the teachings of the Christ because she thought He was a God of the Americans, an enemy of her people. The walls began to shake, there was a thunderous blast, and the next thing she could remember is that she was being pulled from the rubble. Her school was a short distance from Hiroshima. Three hundred students and teachers were killed that day. Caregiver Gladys Hunt writes, "Radiation sickness is a horrible thing. Yoshikosan was hemorrhaging internally and knew she was dying. When it seemed unbearable, she would vacillate between wishing she could die and terror that she might." Her only comfort came in the words of a Psalm that had been made into a hymn she had learned at school, "God is our refuge and strength; in trouble, in trouble, a very present help." The words caused her to reflect on the person of Jesus. She began to pray in the name of Jesus, and each time it would bring her peace. Gradually she became stronger. She was so convinced that God had been her refuge, she shared her newfound faith with her family, who all eventually came to Christ. She then went on to reach many college students in her war-torn country. Ambassadors give what is needed, when it is needed.

Ambassadors for Christ aren't always well known. Christian women, believing God for freedom, worked behind the scenes until the fall of communism came. Women, some with newfound faith, fanned the flame of hope through underground churches in China, the Sudan and other countries hostile against Christianity; women, believing all people were created equal, carried the love of Christ in South Africa, a country torn in two by apartheid. These women are ambassadors who are at great risk at times. While writing this book, I received an email prayer request from a European mission:

> There is a beautiful 15-year-old girl named Saleema in Pakistan who is a Christian. She converted her close friend, 14. This youngster was so excited about Christianity that she told her parents and they killed her! It looks like the 15-year-old is to be publicly executed. We need to send up prayer for this child to give her the strength and resolve to deal with whatever happens to her.

Ambassadors can also be raised up from obscure beginnings. On October 31, 1896, in a Philadelphia slum, a twelve-year-old rape victim gave birth alone. The baby might not have made it, but a neighbor heard the cries and came to the rescue. Ethel wasn't born with a silver spoon in her mouth—she was fortunate to have any spoon at all!

The small child was taken to church where she learned to sing. At five, she gave her first performance in front of that tiny congregation. Ethel ran wild in the streets, practically raising herself. She traveled with a black vaudeville group, then her jazz vocals led her to the famous Cotton Club where she introduced the song, "Stormy Weather," which she said was a picture of her life. Nicknamed Mama Stringbean, Ethel Waters became the first black radio star, then a famed movie actress. But the songs of her youth clung to her soul. In 1957 at a Billy Graham crusade she rededicated her life to God. In the following years her theme song became "His Eye is on the Sparrow" and she traveled with the Billy Graham crusade as a singing ambassador of hope, proclaiming to the millions that God's love can overcome anything life dishes out.[5]

Being an ambassador is a calling.

Os Guinness, in his book *The Call,* says, "First and foremost we are called to Someone (God), not to something (such as motherhood, politics or teaching) or to somewhere (such as the inner city or Outer Mongolia).[6] "There is no calling unless there is a Caller."[7] Romans 1:6-7 clearly supports our call to the *person* of God. "And you also are among those who are called to belong to Jesus Christ. To all in Rome who are loved by God and called to be saints: Grace and peace to you from God our Father and from the Lord Jesus Christ." *You are called!*

His calling is personal: Jesus called the twelve by name. God came to Abram, Jacob and Moses as individuals. The Lord came to Ananias and to Saul. God calls you as a person. He knows you and He calls you.

His calling is permanent: "For God's gifts and his call are irrevocable" (Romans 11:29).

His calling brings purpose: Jesus designated twelve apostles, then He gave them power, authority and a plan. The Holy Spirit said to the early church leaders, "Set apart Barnabas and Saul for the work to which I have called them" (Acts 13:2). Paul was called to be an apostle. (Romans 1:1) We are called to a person, then He gives us our purpose.

His calling leads to a principled life: Paul's prayer in 2 Thessalonians 1:11 gives us a clue on the lifestyle of a called one: "With this in mind, we constantly pray for you, that our God may count you worthy of his calling, and that by his power he may fulfill every good purpose of yours and every act prompted by your faith." What a wonderful partnership! By God's power He will fulfill every good purpose of *yours* and every act prompted by *your* faith. We can experience such freedom in being called. It seems that the only prerequisite is that God count us worthy. So let's look at what we are called to. You and I are called to: come after Christ, take up our cross and follow Christ;[8] according to God's purpose;[9] to be free;[10] to one hope;[11] peace;[12] a holy life;[13] to receive the promised eternal inheritance;[14] to suffer;[15] to inherit a blessing;[16] to be the servant of all.[17]

It seems that one who truly lives out her calling has the internal strength and wisdom to climb the ladder of success quite easily. She will have purpose, hope, freedom, integrity, peace, perseverance and a positive *servant* attitude.

When we have a servant's heart, God can use us. Each of us, serving next to each other, shoulder to shoulder, will move His causes forward. We become living stones, small acts of service laying a foundation expressing the love of Christ: "You also, like living stones, are being built into a spiritual house to be a holy priesthood, offering spiritual sacrifices acceptable to God through Jesus Christ" (1 Peter 2:5). The words *spiritual house* are the same used by Jesus to Peter when Christ said he was building His church on the rock. Each of us are a stone in the spiritual house God is building. *You are a living stone* right now!

God gives three other word pictures to show the value of a servant's heart. In 1 Corinthians 3:9, God explains, "For we are God's fellow workers; you are God's field, God's building." *God's fellow-workers* means we are co-workers of God, thus giving our work dignity, no matter what it is we do. God is the major partner in the enterprise of each life, but He lets us work with Him.

God's field is the picture of our servant role. The field is helpless until the sun shines and until the farmer sows seed and tends to the needs of the crop. I grew up on a farm. My job each summer was to tend our garden. The first few days were the most difficult. We had to rototill the hard, compact dirt, then plant the seed, water and weed. The ground became more and more valuable the more time we invested in it. We are the same way. The more time God invests in us, the more usable we become.

God's building is an architectural picture.[18] When Bill was completing his education, he worked as an architectural draftsman, and I worked to help Bill. No one knew the drawings had walls colored by me. It didn't really matter as long as all the structural specifications were accurate. The same is true all through the building process. Do you know the names of all the carpenters, plumbers, cabinetmakers, cement workers and so on who built the home you live in? Probably not. In the same way, God is saying life still has purpose, even when you don't get the credit for the work.

What Is Needed?

Clayton Hoskinson, an investigator for the Oklahoma Department of Human Services, was directing traffic the day of the bombing. By mid-morning a fine mist had become a driving rain. He was cold, wet, and miserable. An old car, barely running, pulled into the intersection. The driver cracked his window.

"Is this where I'm supposed to drop off the boots?" he asked.

"I had no information about a need for boots. The man had just heard a plea on the radio for steel-toed boots. I told him that we could put the boots with other items, and he rolled down his window and handed me the boots. In the car with him were a woman, an infant and two small children. Taking the boots, I immediately noticed they felt warm on the inside. Looking back into the car I saw the man was wearing no shoes.

"Are these your boots?" I asked.

"Yes." He nodded.

"Sir, no one expects you to give up your own boots," I said as I attempted to hand them back through the window.

With a tear in his eye, he said, "There are people in there who need them worse than I do."[19]

Steven Davis, a corporal with the City Fire Department had ripped his boots while digging for survivors. He was issued a new pair of boots and inside he found a note: "God bless the man who wears these boots, that he may be strong in his search for life." His wife, Tami, framed the note and each time he sees it he thinks, "God bless you too, my friend."[20]

People continued to put people in front of profit. Stores donated items off their shelves. One government worker came to town with 55 cents in his pocket, stayed for over two weeks and in his pocket the day he left was the same 55 cents. The people of the city had taken care of every need out of gratitude for his service and leadership. When the television stations needed a broadcast location, the owner of a computer store donated his store site, shut down his business and refused the lucrative payment the network offered because he didn't want to profit over others' pain. My luncheon friends had spouses who were doctors and those in the medical field worked round the clock for months. Everyone pitched in and did whatever needed to be done.

Harry Allison was called in to help counsel family members who had lost loved ones. A temporary counseling office/morgue was set up at the First Christian Church that was across the street from the bombing. (The church offered its help even though the building had sustained some damage as well.)

> After several hours the families would recover sufficiently to leave the First Christian Church. We did not see them again, with one exception. I had driven from Tulsa that day and noted that all the cars coming toward me had their headlights on, in honor of the victims, and I did likewise. Ten hours later, when I returned to my car, the battery was dead.
>
> A tall black man who was with a white lady approached me, saw that the hood of my car was up, and said familiarly, "Why Doc, you've got car trouble. I'll get my car and get you jump started."
>
> Then I recognized them as a couple I had seen earlier in the church. I said, "It wasn't more than an hour ago you were notified that you lost your two little children...and you want to help me?"
>
> He pulled the photos of his two boys from his breast pocket and said, "We're all in this together. We're all in this together, Doc." [21]

In Oklahoma a revival has taken place. Churches, brimming with people, have built bigger buildings and hired staff because each person is taking the message of hope to those they know. And there is a spirit of sacred somberness that permeates relationships. I experienced it firsthand on my trip to Edmond.

There is a singular focus that has captured the hearts of the people I met. In their ears ring verses like, "What good is it for a man to gain the whole world, yet forfeit his soul?" (Mark 8:36), "Just as man is destined to die once, and after that to face judgment"

(Hebrews 9:27) and "Salvation is found in no one else, for there is no other name under heaven given to men by which we must be saved" (Acts 4:12).

New Lenses

In the races for the hearts and souls of humankind, many things pale in importance when looked at through the lens of eternity. The bathroom that needs a fresh coat of paint falls further down the list when you look at people in your neighborhood through "forever" eyes. The imperfect husband, flaws and all, looks pretty terrific when you consider the alternative of never having him around again. Washing dishes and diapers and driving children to activities that build their lives become holy acts in light of eternity.

Bill Bright, the founder of Campus Crusade for Christ, considers any time he is with someone more than a few minutes as a divine appointment. We have all eternity to praise Him, sing to Him and fellowship with believers, but we only have this short life to tell others about Him and the plan He offers to them. God could have taken each of us directly to heaven the moment we received His grace and love, but instead He chose to leave us here. The stakes are high in this game of life. Each of us will stand before God and give an account. God's main priority on that day will be, "Do you know Me? Have you accepted My Son into your life as a payment for your imperfections?" Millions and millions of people have yet to hear the good news of God's great love in a way they can understand and accept. We are His voice to a lost and dying world. Today might seem like any other ordinary day, but so did April 19, 1995 in Oklahoma City.

Since college I have tried to make all my decisions based on a single question, "What will this do to bring people to Jesus?" Sometimes getting a van has been a strategic move so that I can drive more children and teens to events to hear about God or grow in Christ. We built our home with evangelism in mind—a larger living room and kitchen for hospitality. But other times, I know deep in my heart that it is me who wants Waverly print wallpaper, not God. It is me who desires a new outfit when God wants a missionary wife to have that money. As I weigh out my motives now, 168 faces from Oklahoma City flash across my mind.

And the face of my friend Diane. Diane and I were both on the gymnastics team, the cheer squad and in dance club. Often, if I wasn't with my sister, Deney, I was with Diane.

At my 20-year high school reunion, the names of all those who had died in my class were read. Among those were a young man I had dated, one my sister had dated, a friend from dance class. I recognized nearly everyone on the list, and I remembered the moments when God had prompted me to relate to each of them my personal story of faith.

I remember the excuses well: *God, what if they reject me? What if I lose them as a friend? What if they ask me questions and I don't know the answer? What if they laugh? What if they just aren't interested?* I asked God all those questions—and more. I longed for a plausible excuse not to share my faith. I tried the *I'm too busy, God,* the *I don't know enough, God* and the spiritual, *I'm sure someone else would do a better job.* I even tried the *I'm not sure it's the right time, God* excuse, but the still, small voice kept nudging me forward. In each case, I said yes to God and stepped out and shared my story of how He radically redeemed my life and the hope He offered each of these friends. One by one I talked to them. Some responded right away, some I don't know how they eventually responded, all I know is that God asked and I nodded and obeyed.

God asked me to share my faith with my cheerleading friends from high school. Only a couple came to my house that day. I felt like I'd failed Him somehow. I must have, since the turnout was so small. Diane had called and said she wanted to come but had to work, so I set up a lunch appointment with her. Over lunch I shared Christ the only way I knew how—I read her the *Four Spiritual Laws*. Diane wanted to make a choice to have Christ come into her life that day but she was afraid. She was living with a young man, and she didn't think he'd like her anymore if she got religious. When I explained it wasn't a religion, it was a relationship, she said she'd think about it. And she was true to her word.

I'd taken Diane to church with me a few times in high school, and on and off during those early college years we connected. Sometimes she'd come to a special event at church, sometimes we'd just talk. We were at each other's weddings (she married that young man she had been living with).

But a series of moves in and out of town for each of us made our relationship hit and miss over the next several years. At the ten-year reunion we connected again. Her first marriage had ended and I could tell she was hurting. She was out of a job and pregnant with no husband in sight. We talked for quite a while that night. "Diane, God has a wonderful plan for your life and I'd be glad to help you find it. God loves you. He wants the best for you, but you need to take the step and ask Him into your life."

She had a lot of questions so we began to write back and forth. She was a single mom trying to get her life back on track. I sent a baby gift when her little one arrived and a congratulations card when she got a new job. She wanted to know more about God so I sent her things I thought could help her make the decision to come to the loving God who had created her. Then the letters suddenly stopped. I wrote and my letters were returned by the post office. I wondered if I had done something wrong.

At the next reunion, I found out why the letters stopped. Diane had been driving home after a long day at her new job. She drove her car off an exit embankment. She left two small children.

I told my brother about my friend Diane after the reunion that night. Bret pointed to the late night TV news. Pictures of Princess Diana's crumpled car blazed across the screen. Diane and Diana had a calendar jammed with important activities and plans, but the most important choice they needed to have made was a choice to give God the reins of their hearts. Only God knows their choice for sure.

But on the night of my 20-year reunion, I experienced something I will never forget. I felt like my life had pleased God. The fragmented pieces of my life fell into place. As the names of my dead classmates were read in a moment of silence, I was humbled that me, a woman who began life as a trembling, insecure child had been so transformed that at a point in time, when it mattered most, I'd said yes to God and shared Him.

I wish I could say that I always say yes when I feel that nudge from eternity. But I do say yes much more often because those classmates' names and those faces and stories from a chain link fence in Oklahoma City are etched on my heart and my mind. I believe that God wants to help pull the pieces of our lives together so we don't feel so fragmented and stressed. But I *know* that the most important piece, a corner piece that sets the puzzle in place and helps it all fall together, is how my heart responds to life when I place the grid of eternity over the faces I pass each day. When I look at people and life's tasks through *forever eyes*, I gain perspective and clarity. Things that I thought were so important, so vital, fall into the background. Other times, things that at first glance seem insignificant can grow in significance under the microscope of heaven.

There was a woman, new to our congregation, who battled cancer for many years. Marcia was sick the entire time I knew her. I went to see her in a tiny condo. I knew she continued to work, even through the pain. Her world seemed small. When she passed away, I thought, *I should really go to her funeral. There might not be that many people there. It is even more painful for the family when few people come to a funeral.* So although I didn't know Marcia well, I went. As I drove into the parking lot I had trouble finding a space. As the funeral proceeded, my husband opened up the mike for people in the congregation to share. Person after person streamed to the front to share how one woman, a woman who smiled through the pain of cancer every day for over ten years, had touched their lives. Most had never had a spiritual conversation until they had met her. But Marcia listened. She listened to crazy questions, she listened to breaking hearts, she listened to some people who may never have been listened to before—and she had made a difference.

Heart Ablaze

Every fall in California we have hot dry winds called the Santa Ana winds. When they blow for any length of time, the risk of brush fire goes up. One evening I noticed that a brush fire that had started earlier that day was now cropping the hill tops that surround our church building. It was still miles away, so I went inside to set up for a Bible study I was leading. I had been watching the news all day. People and animals were being evacuated from all the cities around ours. The wind had been carrying the fire away from our city—until that evening.

I again stepped outside to survey the situation as the women began to arrive for the study. We quickly gathered together and decided that what God wanted us to do that night was not study the Bible, but put it into action. I took our church phone directory and we divided up names so that we could call and check on those living in the area, especially our senior church members. We were to inform them of the wind shift, offer evacuation help, and information on emergency shelters. Most of the women at the study also offered their homes. I paged my husband and our church soon became an emergency evacuation shelter. Bill manned the shelter, aiding anyone in need all night long, while I manned the phone like a dispatcher, relaying information to families who had been separated and friends checking on loved ones in the area. Then every 20 minutes or so, I called a few friends who lived at the ridge across a small lake from the fire. And I prayed. Neither Bill nor I slept that night, but we didn't care. People were safe, and that was all that mattered.

As we drove and surveyed the damage the fire had made, Bill and I couldn't help but notice an amazing site. Two wooden crosses survived the blaze when houses, brush and trees had not. They seemed to be a beacon of hope and guidance to our community, a reminder of what really matters most in life: *people and their relationship to God.*

The Gift

It was 3 A.M. and cold, windy and wet as Police Lieutenant Jim Spearman stood at the perimeter of the bombing site. Because the weather was so bad, the leaders of the search and rescue team were taking turns standing guard outside. Jim noticed three people standing just north of the barricade: a boy in his mid-teens, a younger girl and a woman. He thought it was very strange that on a night like this and at that time of the morning anyone would be out and about. He approached the group. The boy walked forward and asked Jim if his younger sister could talk to him. The woman prompted the little girl who appeared to be about nine. The little girl held a well-worn teddy bear and asked, "Could you give this to one of those babies in the hospital?"

The woman explained that the little girl hadn't been sleeping well since the bombing and was very concerned about the child victims. She had awakened up about an hour before and asked if she could go to the bomb site. The bear had been given to her for her first birthday.

Jim told her he would take the teddy bear to the Salvation Army post and they would make sure that one of the children in the hospital got it. The little girl held out her beloved teddy bear. Jim leaned down and asked, "What's your name?"

Her reply: "That's not important."[22]

Lord, give me the heart of this little girl. May I hold out all that is valuable to me and allow You to use it. May people see You, not me. It's 9:02 in our world everyday. Give me forever eyes.

❋ ❋ ❋

Putting the Pieces Together

Brainstorm a list of ways that what you own could be used to bring people information on who Jesus is. Make a list of people you know that don't know Christ yet. Next to each name brainstorm a list of their interests and felt needs. Is there a tangible way you could begin taking Jesus' love to those on your list? Now think of your community. Who are the people at highest risk in your town? Is there a way you could impact just *one* of those lives?

Study Guide

*T*his section is designed for the woman who wants to go to a deeper place with God. Each chapter will have a weeklong assignment followed by small group discussion questions. The assignment may be one question with many facets, or it may be several questions. As you work on digging out a few new truths each day on that topic, you'll discover God has led you through His Word so that you have a fuller, deeper and richer view of the chapter's topic. You can then choose to facilitate or participate in a small group that meets once a week and discusses the chapter, the *Putting Together the Pieces* assignment and the *Deeper Place* adventure with God. You may decide to do the activities and discuss them with a trusted friend, mentor, daughter, daughter-in-law or a spouse. The questions will simply help facilitate a discussion.

Chapter 1: Finding Your Place in His Plan

A Deeper Place:

Read the book of Ruth. In chapter one, note the deep pain Naomi must have felt. What was the cause of her pain? What is the pain in your life right now? Often, for women, our pain is connected to our self-concept or those vital relationships that feed our view of ourselves. Naomi was so depressed, angry and hurt that she even changed her name to outwardly mark the bitterness she felt inwardly. Naomi made a very important choice in chapter one. She went back, back to the place she knew God would meet her, back to a place people would point her to God, back to a place she knew a source of provision would be for her physically, emotionally and spiritually. When life gets confusing, go back. Where are those places you know you heard God speak into your life? If you are feeling used up, or unappreciated or negative about your life, think of a time when you felt the pleasure of God. Close your eyes. Think of a time when you felt you rested in Him. I think one of the reasons swimming is so therapeutic for me is that when things got rough at my house while I was growing up, I would head out to the back pasture and take my Bible and sit, dangling my feet into the cool creek water and I'd read, pray and talk to God. It was my personal oasis. I sensed God's pleasure as I sat and enjoyed His presence. I would encourage you to find a place where you can go to spend time alone with God when you are stressed out. Make it a place where you can remove yourself from any surrounding distractions. Make it a place where you can come to Him alone to share what is on your mind and heart. He tells us to come to Him when we are weary and heavy-laden and He'll give us rest. (Matthew 11:28-29) The key idea is to surrender. Give up your yoke for the one He has designed for you. What are you carrying that feels too heavy? What negative thoughts about yourself are you hearing that you'd like to have Him replace? Do you long to hear His applause, feel His approval? In a quiet time, read the following verses, then ask yourself, *Since God is already doing all these things for me, will He not meet my needs now?* (Luke 15:10, John 14:2-3, Matthew 11:28-30, Revelation 21–22). Write a letter to Jesus. Tell Him all the heavy, negative things in the yoke you've been carrying. Tell Him how you felt as you surrendered, as you read the verses. Tell Him what you'd like to see happen in your life as a result of this study.

Questions to Pull the Pieces Together:

1. Think of the last compliment you received. What was it for? Was it an external compliment, like "Nice dress!" or "Your hair looks great!" or was it an internal compliment of your character like, "You are so thoughtful" or "You are such a faithful friend." Try to describe how you feel when you are given each kind of compliment.

2. Talk about your answer to the *Putting the Pieces Together* assignment: How would you describe a woman "who has it all"? How is the description different from your life right now? Do you think it is possible to "have it all"? Why or why not? Describe a time when you compared yourself to someone else or your life to her life. When was it? How did you feel as a result of comparing? Over the next several days read the verses about handling envy and jealousy. Proverbs 14:30, Proverbs 23:17,

Proverbs 24:1-2, 1 Corinthians 13:4, Titus 3:3-8, James 3:13–4:3, 1 Peter 2:1-3, Romans 13:13-14, 1 Corinthians 3:3-9, 2 Corinthians 12:20–13:8, Galatians 5:20-25, Romans 12:14-21. Come up with a new plan to use when you are tempted to compare. Explain how you will handle those negative feelings the next time they arise.

3. What is your definition of significance? This chapter makes the case that if you see yourself from God's perspective, you will have a more accurate view of what is significant, of what pleases God. Why do you think knowing how God sees you will impact your thinking in the coming weeks?

4. Do you have a specific area that you feel disappointed in, or do you think specific people are disappointed in you right now? Pray with someone and commit those areas to God for His care as you work your way through this book.

Chapter 2: All the Wrong Places

A Deeper Place:

Let's look at a true/false comparison. We'll start with false.

False: Read the entire book of Ecclesiastes. Solomon, the wisest man in history, chose to not believe God for his source of significance. Underline and mark false sources of significance in the margin of your Bible with an "F" for false. List areas of false significance you see in Solomon's life. What are the negative results for each area? What was Solomon's overall state of mind as a result of embracing false sources of significance? Which source of false significance are you most tempted to rely on instead of God? Are there any words of wisdom from Solomon that can help you when you are tempted to embrace a false source of significance?

True: Create your own love letter from God. First list any known weaknesses, foothold or sources for false significance you have embraced. Write down key words that describe these areas. Now next to each, write a few key words that are the opposite of these negative words. Look up verses in the Bible using the positive words. Try to find verses that describe God with terms similar to the positive traits listed. Choose your favorite five to ten verses and string them together. If you'd like, personalize the verses so the message seems to be coming straight from God to you. (See the example in the *Putting the Pieces Together*. Also look at Lisa's affirmations below.)

Psalm 118:1, 8-9
Give thanks to the LORD, for he is good; his love endures forever.

It is better to take refuge in the LORD than to trust in man.

It is better to take refuge in the LORD than to trust in princes.

Psalm 121:7-8
The LORD will keep you from all harm—he will watch over your life; the LORD will watch over your coming and going both now and forevermore.

Psalm 52:8
But I am like an olive tree flourishing in the house of God; I trust in God's unfailing love for ever and ever.

Proverbs 8:17
I love those who love me, and those who seek me find me.

Mark 11:24-25
Therefore I tell you, whatever you ask for in prayer, believe that you have received it, and it will be yours. And when you stand praying, if you hold anything against anyone, forgive him so that your father in heaven may forgive you your sins.

Luke 6:27-28, 35-36

But I tell you who hear me: Love your enemies, do good to those who hate you, bless those who curse you, pray for those who mistreat you. But love your enemies, do good to them, and lend to them without expecting to get anything back. Then your reward will be great, and you will be sons of the most high, because he is kind to the ungrateful and wicked. Be merciful, just as your father is merciful.

Luke 6:37-38

Do not judge, and you will not be judged. Do not condemn, and you will not be condemned. Forgive, and you will be forgiven. Give, and it will be given unto you.

Questions to Pull the Pieces Together:

1. What are the common sources for significance you see promoted on television and in magazines? How does the media make you feel, significant or insignificant? How? Why?

2. Think back on how you were raised. Were there any children's stories, either positive or negative, that helped form your identity? Any things your family told you that formed a misconception of significance in your thinking?

3. What area of false significance are you most vulnerable to believing and embracing?

4. Considering all the examples in the chapter and the example of Solomon, what is the outcome if one continues to embrace false sources of significance?

5. If you'd like, share your finished assignment: *From God's Heart to My Own.* How has it impacted you so far?

Note: You may want to have some diagnostic tools available for women, for example: *Overcoming the Dark Side of Leadership*; *Steps* to *Freedom in Christ* resource booklet. Even a personality test, like *Personality Puzzle* or the *DISK* test can help identify weaknesses women may not want to recognize but need to. These resources can be obtained at the addresses below:

Overcoming the Dark Side of Leadership, Baker Books, P.O. Box 6287, Grand Rapids, MI 49516-6287

Personality Inventory, CLASS, P.O. Box 66810, Albuquerque, NM 87193

Steps to Freedom in Christ guide, Regal Books, 2300 Knoll Dr., Ventura, CA 93003

DISK test, Personality Insights, P.O. Box 28592, Atlanta, GA 30358

Idea: Combine chapters 2 and 3 and give them out over a holiday break or give women two weeks to complete the message *From God's Heart to My Own* assignment.

Chapter 3: A Place in the Son

A Deeper Place:

Read the story of King Saul's life (1 Samuel 9–16; 18–19; 23:7-26; 31:1-6). Try to diagram his downward progression. What key decisions did he make that propelled him in such a destructive pattern?

How about you? Can you identify your dark side and what will happen if you don't address it, keep it in check or grow in victory over it?

Questions to Pull the Pieces Together:

1. Name some modern-day leaders, stars or celebrities that have not dealt with their baggage, their dark side. What is the result you are seeing in their lives?

2. "Our past influences our future." How do you think your upbringing or your own past choices have affected how you see yourself today?

3. What encouragement did you gain from learning that God already sees your imperfections and still loves you? How does this motivate you to want to open up your heart and allow God to grow you up in those imperfect areas?

4. Which *Putting the Pieces Together* assignment did you complete? How do you feel now that you have taken a step forward to address this area?

Chapter 4: A Place of Confidence

A Deeper Place:

Embracing His Choosing: Read these verses on being chosen. Are there any new insights or applications you can make that will help you in your life this week?

John 13:18	Colossians 3:12
Acts 22:14	1 Thessalonians 1:4
Romans 8:33	James 2:5
Romans 11:5	1 Peter 1:2
Ephesians 1:11	1 Peter 2:9
Colossians 1:27	

Failure from God's perspective: Read the following verses on failure. What causes failure in God's eyes and how does God handle it? How does this help you handle failure?

Matthew 26:41	Hebrews 4:11
Luke 8:13	2 Peter 1:10
Romans 3:23	2 Peter 3:17

1 Corinthians 10:12   Jude 1:24

1 Timothy 6:9

Questions to Pull the Pieces Together:

1. What kind of envelope do you think you are?

2. What do you think keeps you from being God's envelope?

3. Do you have a method for sharing His hope that you are comfortable with? (As in the Four Laws, The Bridge, the Roman Road, the wordless book or bracelet of different colors that remind you of the parts of the gospel message.) Visit a Christian bookstore and find a tool that you are comfortable using to share about your relationship with God. (Bring it to the small group.)

4. Did you learn anything that will help you handle criticism?

5. What did you learn that will help you handle the fear of failure or recovering from failure?

6. Think of someone who could use the message of hope, put something in an envelope and mail some encouragement from God to someone this week.

(Note: If you are facilitating a group, this is a good week to remind people not to use real names or full names when describing circumstances that might put the person in a less than positive light.)

Chapter 5: Everything in Its Place

A Deeper Place:

Below are some verses about time. What new insight or reminder of truth can you glean from each?

Genesis 1:3	1 Corinthians 4:5
Psalm 75:2	Galatians 6:9
Psalm 145:15	1 Peter 5:6

Ecclesiastes 3:1-8,11,17   Ephesians 5:15-16

Ecclesiastes 8:5-6

Look up the following verses that contain the words vapor or mist. From the use of the word vapor or mist, what can you learn about the brevity of life from these verses? Proverbs 21:6, Isaiah 44:22, Hosea 6:4 and 13:3.

Look at the Ecclesiastes section, which says there is a time for everything. See if you can translate its meaning into a modern day example. For example: "A time to reap" might mean a time to collect the paycheck or bonus. Mark the ones you have already experienced.

Questions to Pull the Pieces Together:

1. According to a 1996 article in *Health* magazine, the average woman today has a life expectancy of 79 years. How many years does this leave you if you are "average"? How does this make you feel?

2. How does knowing we are mist, free you and your thinking? How does it change your To Do list?

3. What legacy do you want to leave? What do you want said about you at your funeral?

4. If you'd like, read your personal mission statement. How do you think this will help you make choices in the future?

Chapter 6: A Precious Place

A Deeper Place:

Read these verses about our inheritance in Christ, our place in His family and our place in the promise. How does knowing all this affect your view of yourself?

Galatians 3:18   Colossians 3:23-24

Galatians 4:7   Hebrews 9:15

Ephesians 1:13-14,18-23   Hebrews 12:14-17

Ephesians 5:5   1 Peter 1:3-7

Colossians 1:12

God cares for you. The example of His care of you as being more valuable than birds, lilies and the grass are just a glimpse of how well He knows you. Read Psalm 139. What else does God know?

Questions to Pull the Pieces Together:

1. When are you most likely to feel taken for granted? What kicks off that feeling and how have you handled it in the past?

2. Is there something from this chapter that encouraged you as you saw your value from heaven? How can this affect the way you react when you feel you are not being valued here on earth?

3. How do you feel when you realize how well God knows you?

4. Because God values us, He wants us to make the most of opportunities He sends our way. What are opportunities you could take advantage of each week that would give you a more positive view on life? For example, Christian radio, quiet times, conversations with friends or children. How can you take advantage of something in your own backyard this week?

5. The closing example was of a woman who didn't sit around thinking about what she couldn't do, instead she made a list of what she could do and she created an opportunity. Describe a time you created an opportunity or describe something you can do and then ask God to help bring that about.

Chapter 7: A Positive Place

A Deeper Place:

From the chapter, look at the "God's Will Made Clearer" verses again. If your Bible lists cross-references for each verse in this section, look them up and write a one-or two-word synopsis that will help you remember what God wants from your life. By reading cross-references, you can gain a broader perspective on a subject. For example: Romans 12:1-2 talks about sanctification. Reading cross-references can shed an overall light of what a sanctified life might look like, especially when you follow the chain from verse to verse to verse, like clues to a treasure.

Try to create a set of 2-3 questions for each verse in the "God's Will Made Clearer" list. It can become like a thermometer, checking your spiritual temperature and attitude toward God. For example: I am sanctified or set apart, so I ask myself, "Am I guarding what I see, hear and participate in so that the flame of light in me is fanned instead of extinguished?"

Questions to Pull the Pieces Together

1. Which tool of Satan's guilt works best on you?

2. How can knowing you are salt and light help to combat the tool?

3. When do you have the hardest time maintaining your personal healthy boundaries?

4. List the top ten people who have earned more right to your time. What is one boundary you can set that will ensure they have greater access to you? For example: A personal assistant can put calls from your kids through to you no questions asked. You can get an alpha pager that *only* your kids or your spouse can use to reach you.

5. What did you learn about God's voice that can help you discern between bad guilt and good conviction?

Chapter 8: The Resting Place

A Deeper Place:

Read the verses below about the temple Solomon built for God. For each reference listed, write a two- to-five-sentence synopsis that reminds you of what the temple is or how it is to be treated.

1 Kings 5:3-6	1 Kings 5:13-18
1 Kings 6:1-38	1 Kings 7:13-51
1 Kings 8:1-66	

What was God's response?

1 Kings 9:1-9

2 Chronicles 2–7 cross-references this same event. Are there any new or different insights from this passage?

How do these verses impact the way you see yourself, knowing that you are referred to as the temple of the Holy Spirit?

Read these verses on the Sabbath. Make a brief note of what information is in the verse. Are there any lifestyle changes you want to make as a result?

Exodus 16:23, 25-26	Exodus 31:14-16
Leviticus 16:31	Leviticus 23:3, 32
Leviticus 25:4	Isaiah 58:13-14
Matthew 12:1-12	John 5:1-17

David was a man whose life was stressful. How do the Psalms describe rest?

Psalm 16:9	Psalm 55:6
Psalm 62	Psalm 91
Psalm 116	

What did Jesus say about rest?

    Matthew 11:28-29   Mark 6:31

What do the New Testament authors have to say about the way to handle heavy burdens, anxieties and stress?

    Acts 15:25-29   2 Corinthians 11:9, 12:13-14

    1 Thessalonians 2:9   2 Thessalonians 3:8

    Hebrews 13:17   1 Peter 5:7

    Philippians 4:6

Are there any commonalities between what David, Jesus and the other authors said?

Questions to Pull the Pieces Together

1. What causes you stress?

2. Knowing you are the temple of God, are there any bad habits you need to quit or good habits you need to start?

3. Which gift do you need to most give yourself permission to receive? (Emotional connection, contentment, physical care, prayer, celebration or hope?)

4. Share some things off your personal celebration list. Choose one to do today. If you did any last week, how did it make you feel? Why?

5. Did you learn anything from the Deeper Place that will impact your lifestyle?

6. Choose an accountability partner that will ask you everytime she sees you in the next month, "Are you taking care of the temple?"

Chapter 9: The Place that Holds the Key

A Deeper Place:

In the section below, mark every reference to who Jesus is with a cross. Mark every reference to who Jesus says you are with a heart. Underline all references to remain, stay, abide. Circle any promises or results of remaining, abiding, etc. What new insight or reminder did this activity bring to your mind?

John 15:1-16

"I am the true vine, and my Father is the gardener. [2] He cuts off every branch in me that bears no fruit, while every branch that does bear fruit he prunes so that it will be even more fruitful. [3] You are already clean because of the word I have spoken to you. [4] Remain in me, and I will remain in you. No branch can bear fruit by itself; it must remain in the vine. Neither can you bear fruit unless you remain in me.

[5] "I am the vine; you are the branches. If a man remains in me and I in him, he will bear much fruit; apart from me you can do nothing. [6] If anyone does not remain in me, he is like a branch that is thrown away and withers; such branches are picked up, thrown into the fire and burned. [7] If you remain in me and my words remain in you, ask whatever you wish, and it will be given you. [8] This is to my Father's glory, that you bear much fruit, showing yourselves to be my disciples.

[9] "As the Father has loved me, so have I loved you. Now remain in my love. [10] If you obey my commands, you will remain in my love, just as I have obeyed my Father's commands and remain in his love. [11] I have told you this so that my joy may be in you and that your joy may be complete. [12] My command is this: Love each other as I have loved you. [13] Greater love has no one than this, that he lay down his life for his friends. [14] You are my friends if you do what I command. [15] I no

longer call you servants, because a servant does not know his master's business. Instead, I have called you friends, for everything that I learned from my Father I have made known to you. [16] You did not choose me, but I chose you and appointed you to go and bear fruit—fruit that will last. Then the Father will give you whatever you ask in my name.

Questions to Pull the Pieces Together

1. Can you think of a time when the fragrance of obedience impacted your life? Share it with the group.

2. What did you learn about the priority of the Word of God and its link to obedience?

3. Which Bible study method do you want to try so that God's word will be layered into your life?

4. Can you think of a time when either your sinful actions or someone else's resulted in "stinkin' thinkin' "? Can you give an example of an outrageous saying or discussion that resulted because the person (you or another) wasn't walking in obedience?

5. When is it most difficult for you to obey?

6. Share your feelings about this phrase, "accountability only works if someone has a desire to obey." Agree or disagree and why?

7. Is there an area you feel the need to take your thoughts captive before it turns into "stinkin' thinkin' "? Share this with one other member and pray for each other.

Chapter 10: Places of the Heart

A Deeper Place:

In Acts 1:8 it says: "But you will receive power when the Holy Spirit comes on you; and you will be my witnesses in Jerusalem, and in all Judea and Samaria, and to the ends of the earth."

We are witnesses of who Jesus is. Read about John the Baptist in John 1. What can you learn from John that can apply to your life today?

The epistles contain many references to light. Read the verses below and write who or what is the light and its purpose. (Romans 13:12; 2 Corinthians 4:4; 2 Corinthians 6:14; Ephesians 5:8-14; 1 Thessalonians 5:5; Hebrews 10:32; 1 Peter 2:9; 1 John 1:7, 2:9-10.)

Questions to Pull the Pieces Together:

1. Describe the people who might see you as an ambassador. Brainstorm ways to be a more effective ambassador to them. (Learn their language, visit their homes, learn their needs, etc.)

2. Choose one person and one way to be an ambassador and begin praying for and scheduling time for that one individual.

3. How can you gain forever eyes for your world? What will help remind you of the priority of people?

4. Being a woman God can use is really a book about being usable. What attitudes or actions have you changed since beginning this study?

5. How has your self-concept changed? Which "You Are" was most meaningful to you and why?

6. How do you think seeing yourself more accurately, from God's point of view, helps you make better decisions?

Notes

Chapter 1

1. Women of Faith conference, San Diego, CA, July 1998.
2. Lorraine Glennon, ed., *100 Most Important Women of the 20th Century* (Des Moines: Ladies Home Journal Books, 1998), p. 113.
3. John Robinson and Geffrey Godbey, *A Time for Life* (University Park, PA: Pennsylvania State Press, 1997), p. 44.
4. Os Guinness, *The Call* (Nashville, TN: Word, 1998), p. 46.

Chapter 2

1. Dana Demetre, *The Lifestyle Solution Workbook* (San Diego,CA: LifeStyle Dimensions, 1998), p. 43.

2. Ibid., p. 43.
3. 1 Chronicles 29:10-13
4. Psalm 28:7
5. Psalm 121:3
6. 2 Timothy 1:12
7. 1 Thessalonians 5:24
8. 2 Corinthians 1:20

Chapter 3

1. Gary McIntosh and Samuel Rima, Sr., *Overcoming the Dark Side of Leadership: The Paradox of Personal Dysfunction* (Grand Rapids, MI: Baker Books, 1979), pp. 11-12.
2. Ibid., p. 14.

Chapter 4

1. Ephesians 4:30
2. Poor Man's College Quotation search at www.starlingtech.com/quotes/search.html.
3. www.yahoo.com/reference/quotations.
4. Ruth Tucker, Walter Liefeld, *Daughters of the Church* (Grand Rapids, MI: Academie Books, 1987), p. 336.
5. Ibid., p. 337.
6. Ibid., p. 338.
7. J.I. Packer, *Knowing God* (Downers Grove, IL: InterVarsity Press, 1973), p. 37.
8. In "God's Statement of Love to Us" all Scriptures used are from the International Children's Bible, New Century Version, unless otherwise noted.

Chapter 5

1. Patsy Clairmont, Barbara Johnson, Marilyn Meberg, Luci Swindoll, *Joy Breaks* (Grand Rapids, MI: Zondervan Publishing, 1997), p. 241.
2. John Robinson and Geoffrey Godbey, *A Time for Life* (University Park, PA: Pennsylvania State Press, 1997), p. 110.
3. *New Attitudes* web site, www.lifetimetv.com.
4. Kim Clark and Lenore Schiff, "Do You Really Work More?" April 29, 1996, www.pathfinder.com/fortune.html.
5. Ibid., p. 2.
6. Robinson, p. 27.
7. Ibid., p. 236.

8. Ibid., p. xvii.

9. Ibid.

10. Robinson and Godbey, *A Time for Life*, p. 34.

11. Pam Farrel, *Woman of Influence* (Downers Grove, IL: InterVarsity Press, 1996), p. 103.

12. Os Guinness, *The Call* (Nashville, TN: Word, 1998), p. 79.

13. Ibid., p. 45.

14. Dr. Archibald Hart, *Adrenaline and Stress* (Dallas, TX: Word, 1995), p. 138.

15. Ibid., p. 177.

Chapter 6

1. Contributed to "Life in These United States" by Carla J Stark, *Reader's Digest* web page, www.readersdigest.com/rdmagazine/laughline/jokefinder.html.

2. Dilbert, United Feature Syndicate, Inc., 1997 Day Runner, Inc.

3. He Knows My Name by Bill Cantos, John Mandeville, Amy Roth. Copyright 1994 Sausage Bread Music/ASCAP, Hits in Progress/BMI, Will-da-beast Music, BMI. Contact: (615) 847-9626. Used by permission.

4. Galatians 3:26; 4:6

5. Excerpt from web page of Bethune-Cookman College, taken from "Bethune-Cookman College 1904-1994: The Answered Prayer to a Dream," www.bethune.cookman,edu/welcome/founder/founder.html.

6. Lorraine Glennon, ed., *100 Most Important Women of the 20th Century* (Des Moines, IA: Ladies Home Journal Books, 1998) p. 20.

7. Andrea Moss, "Woman's heart: Pure sweetness," *Times Advocate* (Jan.23, 1999), pp. B-1 and 6.

Chapter 7

1. Naomi Beard, *Following Christ Beyond Your Cultural Walls,* Women's Ministry Symposium, March 1998, p. 49. For copies contact: Women's Ministry Institute at 626-398-2291.

2. Ibid., p. 50.

3. Ibid., p. 51.

4. Ibid., p. 54.

5. Ibid., pp. 55-56.

6. Miriam Neff and Debra Kingsporn, *Shattering Our Assumptions* (Minneapolis, MN: Bethany House, 1996), pp. 29-30.

7. Brenda Hunter, *Where Have All the Mothers Gone?* (Grand Rapids, MI: Zondervan, 1982), pp. 92-93.

8. Ibid., p. 90.

9. Lauri McIntyre, NEWIM conference, Riverside, CA, February 5, 1999

Chapter 8

1. Tom Peterson, *Living the Life You Were Meant to Live* (Nashville, TN: Thomas Nelson, 1998), p. 201.
2. Pastor to Pastor, *Budgets and Burnout*, audiotape vol. 1, 1993. Focus on the Family, Colorado Springs, CO 80995
3. Dr. Archibald Hart, *Adrenaline and Stress* (Dallas, TX: Word Publishing, 1995), p.12.
4. Personal interview, February 1, 1999.
5. Dean Ornish, M.D., *Love and Survival* (New York, NY: HarperCollins Publishers, 1998), p. 25.
6. Ibid., p. 29.
7. J.S. House, K.R. Landis, and D. Umberson, "Social Relationships and Health," *Science*, 1998, p. 241:540-45.
8. L.G. Russek and G.E.Schwartz, "Perceptions of Parental Caring Predict Health Status in Midlife: A 35-Year Follow Up of the Harvard Mastery of Stress Study," *Psychosomatic Medicine*, 1997, 59 (2):144-49.
9. T.E. Oxman, D.H. Freeman, Jr. and E.D. Manheimer, "Lack of Social Participation or Religious Strength and Comfort as Risk Factors for Death after Cardiac Surgery in the Elderly," *Psychosomatic Medicine*, 1995, 57:5-15.
10. Ornish, p. 53; For information of this research see, D. Spiegel, *Living Beyond Limits: New Hope and Help for Facing Life Threatening Illness* (New York, NY: Times Books, 1993).
11. J.W. Pennebaker, *Opening Up: The Healing Power of Confiding in Others* (New York, NY: William Morrow, 1990), pp. 118-119.
12. Ornish, p. 95.
13. Hart, *Adrenaline and Stress*, pp. 96-97.
14. Ornish, pp. 59-60.
15. Interview with Michael Roizen, M.D., January 12, 1999. The RealAge Company has a web site at www.realage.com.
16. Dana Demetre, *The Lifestyle Solution* (San Diego, CA: LifeStyle Dimensions, 1998), p. 41. (800) 501-BFIT.
17. Ibid., p. 86.
18. Ibid., p. 147.
19. Virtue, *Make Your Home a House of Prayer,* January 1999.
20. USA Today WWW search *Health Magazine*.
21. Send them my way at mliving@webcc.com.
22. Karen Peterson, *A Chuckle a Day Does Indeed Help Keep Ills at Bay*, www.usatoday.com.
23. Ibid.

24. Hart, p. 28.

Chapter 9

1. *Strong's Exhaustive Concordance WordSearch.*
2. Walk Thru the Bible ministries: www.walkthru.org or 800-763-5433.
3. NEWIM conference, February 6, 1999.
4. Ibid.
5. Chosen Women conference, May 1997, Pasadena, CA.

Chapter 10

1. What Would Jesus Do?
2. Underlying source material see *The Teacher's Commentary*, 1983, Scripture Press Publications, Inc., Licensed by Victor Books. See NavPress software.
3. Ibid.
4. Clive Irving, ed., *In Their Name* (New York, NY: Random House, 1995), pp. 46-47.
5. Ruth Tucker, *Stories of Faith* (Grand Rapids, MI: Daybreak Books, 1989), p. 312 and Ethel Waters web page "Colored Reflections."
6. Os Guinness, *The Call* (Nashville, TN: Word, 1998), p. 31.
7. Ibid., p. 20.
8. Mark 8:34
9. Romans 8:28
10. Galatians 5:13
11. Ephesians 4:4
12. Colossians 3:15
13. 1 Thessalonians 4:7
14. Hebrews 9:15
15. 1 Peter 2:21
16. 1 Peter 3:9
17. Mark 9:35
18. Robertson's Word Pictures, WordSearch
19. Tucker, *Stories of Faith,* p. 94.
20. Ibid., p. 96.
21. Ibid., p. 151.
22. Ibid., p. 127.